SACRED VERSES

PART TWO
(THE JOURNEY CONTINUES)

GENE JACKSON

iUniverse, Inc.
Bloomington

SACRED VERSES
PART 2, THE JOURNEY CONTINUES

The views expressed in this work are solely those of the author and do not necessarily reflect the views of the publisher, and the publisher hereby disclaims any responsibility for them.

iUniverse books may be ordered through booksellers or by contacting:

iUniverse
1663 Liberty Drive
Bloomington, IN 47403
www.iuniverse.com
1-800-Authors (1-800-288-4677)

Because of the dynamic nature of the Internet, any web addresses or links contained in this book may have changed since publication and may no longer be valid.

Any people depicted in stock imagery provided by Thinkstock are models, and such images are being used for illustrative purposes only.

Certain stock imagery © Thinkstock.

ISBN: 978-1-4620-6154-9 (sc)
ISBN: 978-1-4620-6155-6 (e)

Printed in the United States of America

iUniverse rev. date: 10/28/2011

To Chris:

". . .for he was like, had he been tried,

to have proved most royal."

and, To David,

the Spartan.

Author's Note

The *Divine Comedy* of Dante Alighieri was written in a strict rhyme scheme of *Terza Rima*. This is feasible in Italian, but is not possible in English. Therefore all of these verses are written in the form of sonnets. By far, the majority are Italian (or Petrarchian), but each chapter ends in one or more Shakespearean sonnets. As far as I am aware this represents the longest sonnet sequence in English literature. The verses are titled as *Sacred*, not in the sense of *Holy* or *Devout*, but following the classical meaning of relating to the spiritual or intellectual universe, instead of the body and the physical world, which would be *Profane*.

The first volume of this sequence represented an exploration of the physical universe in which we live and may be considered equivalent to the *Inferno* of Dante. This second volume is concerned with philosophy or an intellectual attempt to understand this universe. Therefore it could be considered as a parallel to the *Purgatorio* of Dante. The third volume, yet to come, will examine the spiritual aspects of our world and may be regarded as a counterpart to Dante's *Paradisio*.

"Only to gods in heaven
      Comes no old age or death of anything.
            All else is turmoiled by our master, Time.
                  Earth's glory fades,
                        And mankind's strength will go away;
Faith dies, and Unfaith blossoms like a flower.
      And who can find, in the open streets of men
            Or secret places of his own heart's love
                  One wind blow true forever?"

Sophocles

"Oedipus at Colonnae"

"But soon we too shall die,
      And all memory of those we loved will have left the earth,
            And we ourselves shall be loved for a while and then forgotten.
But the love will have been enough;
      All those impulses of love return to the love that made them.
            Even memory is not necessary for love;

There is a land of the living and a land of the dead,
      And the bridge is love,
            The only survival,
                  The only meaning."

T. Wilder

"The Bridge of San Luis Rey"

Volume Two

A CLEAR, WELL-LIGHTED SPACE

Although the universal energy
Which moves the stars, the planets and the sun
Had been explained to me, when that was done,
My place within remained a mystery.
Infinitesimal in size as we
Must seem (to anyone's comparison
With all the universe), what simpleton
Would think I was important, who but me?
The longest span of life one might expect
Is but an instant in the course of time,
We come and stay awhile, then go away,
A short and useless term in retrospect;
Significant as silent pantomime,
We are to God at most a winter's day.

Thus, almost everything can be explained
By principles which are abbreviated
As mathematic formulas, equated
To demonstrate that balance is maintained.
So mass and energy are both restrained
And interactive, both originated
In one split-second, when they were created,
And all became as it was fore-ordained.
And yet, as all the universe evolved,
One space survived, perhaps by God's intention,
Or accident or uncorrected blunder,
A singular enigma unresolved:
The human mind, with one unique dimension,
An infinite capacity for wonder.

I found this difficult to comprehend,
Like Plato's labyrinth, for when I thought
That I had finished all the turns and ought
To come out finally, and to the end,
I found the path I followed to extend
Much further to the future, and distraught,
I saw that all my efforts merely brought
Another challenge which I must transcend.
I thought that knowledge of the world would bring
Enlightenment and peace, instead I found
A course I could not end, or think of winning,
An incompleteness, more than anything.
I looked about and saw familiar ground,
For I was once again at the beginning.

But now, a small pavilion stood ahead,
Just where the path went through an open space,
A pleasant, light and airy summer place
With open sides, but covered overhead.
It was not free, two figures there, instead,
Were waiting patiently, as if in case
I needed someone's guidance to retrace
My course; as I approached the pair, one said:
"You will be welcome here, come, stay awhile,
And tell us of the things that you have learned,
Of quarks and pions, singularity,
The mysteries that you can reconcile,
And some that you cannot, why you've returned,
In search of wisdom and serenity."

He, an older, courtly gentleman,
Was wearing white, a well-pressed linen suit,
Respectful, gracious, with an absolute
 Assurance as the great historian
Of all philosophy, custodian
Of knowledge, music, art, that constitute,
Each one, the highest human attribute,
To civilize us more than science can.
She, the younger, wore a summer dress,
Alert, assertive, never disagreeing,
(But certainly not secretarial);
A lively sprite, she had an effortless
Uncommon grace, a lightness in her being.
And then I heard him call her "Ariel".

Together, equally they seemed content
And calm and self-contained, and quite at ease,
Surrounded now by birds and bumblebees,
Instead of great ideas and eminent
Philosophers and other excellent
Designers and composers; such as these
Had occupied their spirits, now the trees
Stood silently around them, eloquent.
But once again they had been asked to speak
With one who sought enlightenment; somehow,
Their students were reduced to only me.
Responding graciously with their unique
Perspective on our lives, they came, but now
Before beginning, offered me some tea.

The tea and scones were very civilized,
And in the progress of our conversation,
They marveled at my recent education,
Which was intense but rather specialized.
For during tea I briefly summarized
Extensive scientific information
On physics, energy, the world's creation
And mathematics I had memorized.
Then at the end there was an awkward pause,
Around the table, all were hesitant,
As teachers and the student lost alignment;
And then I realized it was because
The schoolboy's thesis was irrelevant,
For he had missed the point of his assignment.

I recognized a small ironic smile
As they remarked to me, quite graciously
That I had learned much more geometry
And astro-physics than they could compile
In all their books, and I could reconcile
The controversies of cosmology
That plagued great scientists through history;
But still, my learning was not versatile.
"Sometime ago, there was a separation
Of basic visions of the universe,
And you have followed one to its conclusion.
Perhaps you did this in anticipation
Of understanding life itself, diverse,
Mysterious, but ending in confusion."

"The road you chose, a very valid one,
Goes back as far as Greece, the Atomists
Believed that all within the world consists
Of particles, and this phenomenon
Alone is real, and by comparison
A universal principle exists,
But only in the mind; for scientists
This represents their highest paragon.
Their mathematics is abstract, equations
Can be erased (except within their minds),
They represent the objects, energy,
And forces which in varied combinations
Are seen and touched and measured, and these kinds
Of things are real, with true validity."

"When Isaac Newton saw his apple fall,
He likely picked it up, and in his hand
He felt its weight and shape, could understand
This object had a presence; it was small,
But if he threw it now against a wall,
Then he could watch its course and see it land,
And hear the sound (perhaps a "splat") demand
Attention from his senses, one and all.
But when he calculated gravity,
(That caused the apple and the earth's attraction),
Momentum, principles of impetus,
These concepts always stayed elusively
Just out of reach; and thus his new abstraction
Would keep them, in his mind, ambiguous."

"When Einstein made his thought-experiment,
The concept was completely in his mind;
And though it changed the world for all mankind
And proved to be a crucial incident
Relating space and time, this excellent
And universal principle confined
Itself to nebulous and undefined
Expanses, only vaguely evident.
This first convention of the universe,
Maintains that objects we can sense alone
Have true reality, assumes reliance
On reason and on logic; to converse,
It needs a mathematic language, known
To all the students of this modern science."

"Now, you have followed that precise tradition
As far as current knowledge will allow,
And almost surely you would disavow
A sense of satisfaction with your mission;
But here we have a second proposition,
Which we believe you should consider now.
The offer is quite free, unless somehow
You feel that you should pay us some tuition."
I noted once again a gentle smile,
That showed their offer to be genuine,
And that no form of payment was expected.
Still, now it seemed that I must reconcile
Myself to more endeavor, to begin
To fill a certain space, so far neglected.

I asked them to continue, to commence
Their explanation of a second way
To think about the world and to portray
Our life as more than mere coincidence.
"We feel that here we have some competence,
We spent our lives attempting to survey
Philosophers (and prophets too), and say
Exactly how they made a difference.
This second pathway started with the Greeks,
With Aristotle, Plato, Socrates,
Who felt that universals had existence
Both in and out of things, and their techniques
Of questions, logic and analyses
Were followed, then and now, with great persistence."

"For their tradition was adopted by
Some theologians, orthodox, deistic
And grades between, who sometimes altruistic,
(But sometimes not), could often fortify
An argument that others would deny.
And all through history there was the mystic
Who labeled all his visions realistic
And used this stratagem to prophesy.
Not only prophets, but the humanist
Philosophers once sought their definition
Of universal truth; reality
If sometimes seeming not to co-exist
With theory, could have a brief audition,
Perhaps to qualify more readily."

"So you can see there are some pitfalls here;
It's always hard to prove erroneous
A concept which may be ambiguous,
But hold a bit of truth, and be sincere.
Philosophy is not as strict and clear
As mathematics, even calculus,
Which by equations, often strange to us
Can make the smallest error disappear.
And yet, in abstract thought the human mind
Is near the pinnacle of great achieving;
If we can filter all the chaff away
And only keep the seeds, then we may find
Profound eternal truth, well worth believing,
And insights more intense than we can say."

"Philosophy, not only inexact
In terms and concepts, has another flaw,
(Which Socrates, among the Greeks, foresaw),
That never caused a prophet to react.
Because ideas and visions are abstract
They are not governed by a common law
Requiring their proponent to withdraw
His overture if not confirmed as fact.
By scientific law, a proof requires
A second independent duplication
Or practical experiment that shows
Objective, not self-serving verifiers.
But where is such secure corroboration
When dealing with the thoughts that men propose?"

"We warn you so that you may be aware
That you are entering a situation
Unlike before, and your affiliation
With men of science will not serve you there.
Now you must independently compare
Assorted schools of thought whose confrontation
Might seem impossible for mediation
Or synthesis, or compromise that's fair.
And yet this is your new assignment now:
To follow human thoughts through history,
Accepting those that seem to you correct,
And merging what your judgment will allow
Into a personal philosophy
Of which you are the only architect."

I knew that it was time for me to leave,
For they had given me an oversight
Of what I would encounter: erudite
Philosophers and thinkers who believe
In absolutes that reason can achieve,
Imagination that is real, despite
The lack of proven models, which unite
And verify the concepts they conceive.
 They both had made their journey long ago,
With efforts both selective and tenacious;
With compromise and fusion, they had reached
An understanding for themselves, although
They knew their role was not (for they were gracious),
To give a judgment on what others preached.

The tea was finished; I went on my way,
Expressing gratitude and deep respect
For both their gifts of time and intellect
Which they had shared with me, their protégé.
And now I felt that I could best repay
Their efforts with a thoughtful, and correct
And diligent endeavor to reflect
Upon the things that I had heard them say.
The personalities that I would meet,
Sincere philosophers and mystics, too,
Would be confusing, contradictory;
But only I could form a balance-sheet
Appropriate for one, myself, that knew
No solid moral authenticity.

I could not tell, (and could *they* even tell?)
If their appearance of serenity
Was due to honest work, completed well,
Endeavors carried out with energy,
Or did it stem from their secure relation,
Devoted and assured for many years,
Constructed on the sturdiest foundation:
Companions, friends and partners, always peers.
A gentle incline led me to the crest,
And there I turned and gazed at where I'd been.
I knew that this would likely be the best
Of sanctuaries I might find again;
The two were in the center of the scene,
Still waiting, still together, still serene.

THE HONEST MAN

I gathered up my strength to go again
Around the circuit I had walked before,
While wondering what thoughts I would explore,
What esoteric mental regimen
I would encounter on my journey, when
I heard a sound, and soon could not ignore
A growing and cacophonous uproar
That emanated from a nearby glen.
A multitude of men were gathered there,
(It seemed to me no women were admitted).
There was much talk but little listening,
The noise produced confusion everywhere,
And made it hard to tell who benefited;
Their main activity was arguing.

Then, bearing candles in two candlesticks,
A man approached, who seemed to be somewhat
Apart from all the rest of polyglot
Debaters; these like frantic lunatics
Continued with their multiple prolix
Disputes. He told me: "They will not
Disdain to deafen those within earshot;
Those are the Greeks, discussing politics."
But he was looking for an honest man,
And peered quite deeply in my face, and then
Said: "Oh! well, innocence will do for now,
You are naïve, but no barbarian;
So I will guide you past these mindless men,
As far as truth and honor will allow."

"This is the Agora, you see a clinic
In rudimentary democracy.
The mob assembles, argues aimlessly,
Believes their judgment to be wise, rabbinic;
It truly is ambiguous, Delphinic.
Detached, it is not difficult to see
That equal citizens will not agree
On anything; and so they call me Cynic.
I do not quarrel with their right to speak,
And in debate, I probably would win;
But I object to how they agonize
And play eternal verbal hide-and-seek
While practicing a useless discipline,
Creating laws I do not recognize."

"I need no law because I harm no one,
And since I own and keep no property,
There is no way that one could steal from me.
The way to be content is first to shun
All property and wealth, when this is done
Sincerely and completely, one must be
Content; with pleasure gone, the soul is free,
The least among us is our paragon.
A story that is true will show the worth
Of living with austerities like these:
One day the king, the young and great commander,
And ruler over more than half the earth
Passed by, and wished he was Diogenes;
I did not wish that I was Alexander."

"He asked what he (the king) could do for me,
And I advised that he not block the sun.
Its hearty warmth, that any simpleton
Would value, was the greatest gift that he,
So powerful, with all his courtesy
Could give; so having nothing, needing none,
This was the ultimate comparison
To one who ruled the world, unhappily.
And now, I think the time for you to choose
Is present if you feel that I am right.
Denial and restraint promote the whole
Of virtue in a modest life, to lose
Possessions is to gain a true insight;
Desire and envy eat away the soul."

"You need not always do without these things,
Like houses, clothes and food, but must not care
About them, you can sleep just anywhere;
A tub will do as well on evenings
When it is warm, an empty wine vat brings
A fragrance to your rest a millionaire
Would envy, taking charity is fair
And upright, if without the grovellings.
Explaining origins of life reveals
A mental weakness which I overcame;
I have a silly friend who always chatters
About the large Ideas and great Ideals,
And Metaphysics, which is just a game,
Since ethics is the only thing that matters."

"A priest (perhaps Apollo's) came to me
To tell me of the things the virtuous
Enjoy after death. Then curious,
(Perhaps ill-mannered, too), I asked why he
Along with his disciples did not free
Their souls for early, certain, glorious
Rewards; they all, if truly serious,
Would end their lives, with all alacrity.
In contrast, virtue is its own reward,
The ethical and upright need no gods.
I would suggest, a man can choose his death,
Its time and place, it is not all that hard,
And is legitimate; against the odds,
My method was by holding my own breath."

"But I can see that you are not impressed
With poverty enough to join me.
And it is just as well, I could have guessed,
For all men's spirits are completely free.
Though begging is a thing that I pursue,
Creating moral freedom, here's the rub:
The alms at hand are limited and few,
There's only space for one within my tub.
I'll take you to my Idealistic friend;
Perhaps he'll show you how to reconcile
The hard realities of life and blend
Them all into a universal style."
And that is how I started eagerly
Attending Plato's great Academy.

THE ACADEMY

My shabby friend and guide escorted me,
And even with his manners (unrefined)
He seemed accepted well, and disinclined
To slander those we met, or disagree
With their debates, maintaining dignity.
But he had left his candlesticks behind;
Did he no longer think that he could find
A righteous man, of noble quality?
"No, I have often scanned these men before,
And some of them will have an honest thought
On some occasions; others then will urge
Reflection, to consider and explore
Some other option, which will come to naught,
Then useless compromises will emerge."

"Such is the nature of philosophers;
But I will leave you with the very best,
For I can sense (though you did not request),
That you'd prefer a school of questioners
To public mobs of merely gossipers."
Then he was gone, and I was now a guest
Of foppish students, all were overdressed;
 I had been left among probationers.
This situation left me ill-at-ease,
I had no uniform-like cap or gown,
And I was surely over twice their age.
They stared, as if at aborigines
Or at first glance of some unwitting clown,
Who suddenly is thrust upon the stage.

The Master came, commanding our attention.
We were within a grove, a pleasant place,
But when he took his seat within that space,
His very presence added one dimension.
His moral force and power, by extension
Now seemed to re-align and interlace
The lines of interaction, and erase
The frivolous confusion of pretension.
For like Confucius, who (I heard it said),
By merely sitting in a certain way
Could calm and then control chaotic forces,
Arrival of this teacher brought instead
Of foolish idle chatter, straightaway
His organized and rational discourses.

A major part of his authority
Was his appearance, muscular and tall,
A wrestler's body, unconventional
For one devoted to philosophy.
And he was handsome, even I could see
That some of his success was physical;
But adding to his aura most of all,
The confidence of aristocracy.
His clothes and robe were plain and unaffected,
In contrast to the multicolored crowd.
Simplicity was so atypical
It reinforced the image he projected;
And though his single voice was never loud,
It could be heard quite clearly there by all.

He was a man of forty years or more,
Had been a student until twenty-eight
Of Socrates; but then the winds of fate
And Greek democracy had closed the door
On free philosophy, which heretofore
Had seemed a sanctuary, adequate
To guarantee an open, true debate;
It frightened and depressed him to his core.
For safety and for further education,
He left, and traveled through the world for years,
To Egypt first, and then to Sicily,
And joined Pythagoras, in admiration
Of his new school of educated peers,
A communistic aristocracy.

Yet all equality is not the same,
Since here it seems the neophyte beginner
Was just an outer student, not an inner;
For after years of silence, one became
A privileged full member, with a name,
And in this time, they each became much thinner.
The cause was what they all were served for dinner,
With abstinence and self-control to blame;
He found there were restrictions as to food
(All meat and eggs forbidden, even beans).
Because the Master was a doctrinarian,
Resistance to this diet was subdued;
But strong men cannot live on merely greens,
Nor be a sound and sturdy vegetarian.

Because he was athletic, tall and broad,
He wrestled Milo, lost, then found him cheating,
Not in the match, but earlier, in eating;
Pythagoras's strongest man was flawed
By eating meat for strength, which would defraud
The equal rules by which they were competing.
Thus he decided, following his beating,
That moral inconsistency was odd.
For one could lose by following the rules
Of moral life, but equally could win
By disregarding standards that increase
Disciples' hope of heaven, only fools
Would play a game that had this origin;
And so, with sadness, he returned to Greece.

Among the things he brought with him were these:
Belief that senses (sight and touch) reveal
A world that does exist, but is not real,
In which all things are mere facsimiles.
The perfect forms, produced by syntheses
Within the mind, would create an ideal
External template. He could not conceal
A life-long reverence for Socrates,
But on the great agnostic's doubt he grafted
A faith in universals, and discussed
Utopia, perfection, purity.
His scheme of moral politics was drafted
On social justice, passionate distrust
Of all the mobs, and of democracy.

And by some sense I still cannot explain,
As he surveyed his young and motley crew,
He saw me, realizing I was new.
I wore no ribbons, had no fancy cane,
No blatant badge, yet he could ascertain
I had at least a partial residue
Of basic learning (so an overview
Of long-lost knowledge often will remain).
Then "Sir", he said to me, "would you come here?
For as you know, I am no demagogue,
We learn together here, each one of us,
And as our master, Socrates, made clear
The honest way is by a dialogue;
So let us see what you and I discuss."

And when I went and sat by him, he said:
"We have a saying, 'No one enters here
Who has no mathematics.' It is clear
That you are educated and well-read,
And have been taught geometry. Instead
Of boring lectures, we would love to hear
You speak to us, if you would volunteer
To solve a problem we inherited.
Our younger students, like Demosthenes,
Lycurgus, Aristotle and the rest
Have struggled mightily with this assignment,
And no one votes for their hypotheses."
Then I assured him I would do my best,
And tried to get my mind into alignment.

For I could tell this was some form of test,
Much like fraternity initiation,
Wherein the newest pledge's aggravation
Became the way that bonding was expressed.
And, only superficially their guest,
I was the point of their interrogation,
The path, if not to pure humiliation,
To prove I was inferior at best.
The master spoke and said, "Now to your peers,
Discuss the uniform and ordered motion
Which can be calculated to explain
The movements we observe among the spheres
In heaven, and the planets, how the ocean
Can rise and fall each day, and rise again."

They had no concept yet of gravity,
But then I saw the crucial differences,
For they relied on logic, not on senses,
And sought a universal harmony.
For them, the world they knew, illusory,
Was false though proven, their experiences
Mere copies of the World, if not pretenses;
Distortions of the perfect galaxy.
The question had been asked, now all sat waiting;
The master would confuse the sophomore,
And they had loosed the genie from the bottle.
Their wish was for some elegant debating,
For some had faced these challenges before,
Antiphanes, perhaps young Aristotle.

But now it was my turn, the rest were waiting,
Expecting first that I would misconstrue
The complex question, which upon review
Could not be answered, thereby demonstrating
The fallacy of senses, indicating
Again that only reason was the true
And simple, perfect pathway leading to
A universal form, self-validating.
Declining to provide this satisfaction
Or recognize their "world-in-parallel",
I taught them science, with particulars,
So none could think it fantasy, abstraction.
The first was Thales, who they say once fell
Into a ditch, while gazing at the stars.

And after Thales came Pythagoras
Who thought the universe a living sphere
Whose center was the earth; the stars cohere
From fiery rocks, said Anaxagoras,
The earth from clouds of ether, and from gas.
But all the world, the earth and atmosphere,
Derived from fire and force, will reappear
Through constant change and flux, a great morass.
From Thales' static frozen water, ice,
Young Heracleitas asked how things become,
For "nothing will abide but all things flow;
You cannot step into a river twice,
Since it will never be the same, for some
Cascades will come to you and others go."

Anaximander thought that cylinders
Could represent the earth, somehow suspended
Quite freely in the universe, attended
By circling stars, and these diameters
Of curving orbits were the arbiters
Of universal balance, which depended
On equal distances from earth, extended
To planets, measured by astronomers.
There was the thinker, Anixamines,
Whose principle depended on the air,
From which all else derived; and then the strange
Democritus (the Atomist), Parminides,
Who thought of Unity, and could declare,
"All things are One, and none of them will change."

Now, Epicurus was an Atomist
Like Democritus, he who imitated
Pythagorean rules, and designated
The basic structures, atoms, which consist
Of tiny static modules; these exist
United and intact, and concentrated,
And out of which all life can be created.
But with what force? What is the catalyst?
For Epicureans, the law was chance,
The quantity of matter stays the same,
With none created, none can be destroyed.
The distant gods have no significance,
And grant to men no credit and no blame,
For there are only atoms, and the void.

Accepting principles of sense and matter,
The Stoics added force, which they called *fire*,
Replacing *chance*, the great disqualifier
Of unifying Soul, and which could scatter
The atoms randomly, with noisy clatter
Disturbing silent space. They chose the higher
Harmonic rule; with chaos in the prior,
They sought a Unity within the latter.
And force, directing matter, was alive
And constant, universal, thus divine,
Providing its direction and control.
Although impersonal, it would survive;
For heat and fire give life, and thus define
The Universe, its structure and its soul.

The Skeptics had the ultimate extension
Of what the great agnostic, Socrates,
Explored in each of his analyses,
But taken to the terminal dimension.
They felt the world beyond their comprehension,
All explanations were catastrophes,
A waste of time, for no one ever sees
Things uniformly, this avoids dissension.
And thus they said, "You cannot ever know;
No man can know the world and what is there,
Or whether life has any consequences."
They reveled in their ignorance, and so,
Their search for truth abandoned in despair,
They thus accepted that which fate dispenses.

Up to this point, they heard my argument
Respectfully, and with a close attention.
They murmured their approval at the mention
Of Socrates, but had a different
Reaction to the Skeptics, their dissent
Was impolite to say the least; suspension
Of reason was beyond their comprehension.
In general they thought me competent,
But then they pointed out that I forgot
The basic elements Empedocles
Described: the water, earth, and fire and air;
For even Stoics said the world cannot
Exist without the combinations these
Constituents can form, seen everywhere.

They thought that I had finished my review,
And they should try to fill in several gaps;
Their vigor to correct occurred perhaps
Because I had been teaching what they knew.
Instead of harmony, objections grew,
For each new system finally entraps
Its authors with internal handicaps
And contradictions, proving it untrue.
Into this ferment, they could only draw
On thinkers living very long ago.
They only knew their own contemporary
Endeavors to make sense of all they saw
And all they reasoned; thus they did not know
That what I'd said was just preliminary.

For I had no intent of stopping there;
The Master had produced the impetus
To show my knowledge in a serious
Discussion past the level they could share.
So I began with those who could declare
That Ptolemy was wrong and spurious,
Like Galileo and Copernicus
And all the rest, of whom I was aware.
The list included Tycho Brahe, too,
Johannes Kepler, Digges and Rheticus,
Giordano Bruno of the tragic fate,
Borelli, Bouillard, Hooke and Halley, who
Preceded Newton, and Fabricius,
Who equaled Galileo in debate.

Then on to Newton, with his calculation
Combining distance, mass and gravity
Into a simple concept which can be
Expressed within a singular equation.
And here I could have stopped in this summation,
But with momentum up, the energy
Which I had generated easily
Was not responsive to deceleration.
So on I went to Einstein, who expanded
On all of Newton's concepts, and Lemaitre,
With Oppenheimer, Penrose, Bohr and Hubble,
And Chandrasekhar, who was reprimanded
By Eddington, and Planck the innovator;
Some won a prize, some nothing for their trouble.

From Fermi and from Friedmann in the past
To Penzias and Wilson in the present,
I covered steady states, now obsolescent,
And trans-galactic noise, which by contrast,
Can show expansion, uniform and vast.
My listeners had gone from effervescent
To passive, somnolent, at least quiescent,
And so I ceased my lecturing at last.
It must have seemed to them ridiculous,
For I was speaking in a foreign tongue,
My technical expressions were unique,
My knowledge took me far beyond them, plus
I had forgotten who I was among;
My mathematic language was not Greek.

A silence filled the whole Academy,
For not a single one could understand
My answer to their challenge (which was planned
Primarily to test stupidity).
And now that they could see the irony,
(My explanation had not only scanned
Their universe, but others far more grand),
They owed the stranger an apology.
The Master spoke, still calm and self-assured,
"I stand corrected, sir, you've done quite well.
In tribute now, I have this one suggestion,
(Because your status here has been secured),
That both of us proceed in parallel,
And in your honor I'll retire that question."

"But stay awhile," he said, "And let us find,
Just what significance your world contains;
For you have told us of these grand domains,
Where great opposing forces are combined
To create perfect balance when aligned.
Attraction and repulsion in the planes
Of planetary orbits thus restrains
Disorder, can you see it in your mind?"
And yes, I could, the beautiful ellipse
Of planets orbiting around the sun,
Of particles around their nucleus.
In my imagination, these eclipse
The mundane observations, that when done
And calculated, prove the Marvelous.

And had Johannes Kepler fantasized
On images like these before his laws
Anticipated inverse squares? The flaws
In planetary orbits he revised
(From circle to ellipse), were they devised
Within his mind at first, and then because
His calculations would require a pause,
They only later could be finalized?
A line that joins a planet to the sun
Sweeps equal areas in equal times.
Now, was this symmetry at first a vision
That later, with the computations done
Became a perfect law? Do paradigms
Begin as dreams, with later definition?

Was Galileo's stationary sun
And circling planets first a fantasy?
Did Newton's mind conceive of gravity
Before the apple's fall was fully done?
I pondered on these questions one by one,
And saw the Master gently smile at me,
As if he read my mind. "And now you see,
Ideas to be a true phenomenon.
I do not doubt your proofs or your equations,
Or that the world exists as you have shown,
With objects, elements of many kinds.
But when they change, by death or strange mutations,
The sum of things that you and I have known
Will still exist as perfect in our minds."

"And when your superstrings have ceased vibrating
Thus causing galaxies to involute,
Black holes to form, and every attribute
Within your cosmos starts degenerating,
Then will these changes be invalidating?
Will involution cancel your astute
Equations, calculations, and refute
Your findings which have been so fascinating?
Your theories, if valid, will retain
Eternal truth, through all their permutations.
The central principle alone is real,
And will be so, regardless of the strain
Inaccurate results and estimations
May place upon the absolute ideal."

"Enough of this", he said, "You did not come
These many miles and spend these tiresome years
To joust with me, although it now appears
You are a clever adversary; some
Among my students must be labeled 'dumb',
And others 'rich' (which also interferes
With worthy intellectual careers),
But you deserve a sound curriculum.
Already you have scanned the universe
Far past our limits; whether it is real,
Illusory or false will be resolved
Beyond our time on earth. Let us immerse
Ourselves instead in what our lives reveal
Of abstract Good, and how are we involved?"

Of course he was correct, for I had spent
A great amount of time so far in learning
Mechanics of the universe and earning
A comprehension and an excellent
Appreciation of the firmament.
But was I any wiser now concerning
An existential inquest overturning
A universe that seemed indifferent?
So I agreed that we should now progress
To ways in which the individual
Could find his place, and live a life within
A world of virtue, and without distress.
But this new method should be integral
To all my prior well-earned discipline.

So he began, and said: "Would you agree
That men are born and die, but Man survives?
And so the race goes on through many lives."
I thought that this seemed true; said "Certainly,
Your principle seems obvious to me."
He stated, "Pleasure that a man derives
From beauty may be brief, and this deprives
Each (one and all), of false complacency.
But having seen a flower, like a rose,
I can remember, when it goes away,
The time it gave me pleasure; memory
Prevents the loss of beauty past the close
Of one experience, and can display
An image on the mind, eternally.

"So Beauty lives, despite the brief existence
Of any one particular example;
For if you take a certain rose, and trample
The flower in the ground, the mind's assistance
 Reformulates the image's persistence.
And so the Rose will live, and there are ample
Occurrences, this one is just a sample;
For Beauty is immortal at a distance."
We all agreed with this one metaphor,
Revealing that reality transcends
The individual that does exist
But is not permanent; the guarantor
Of universal qualities depends
Upon the mind of one Idealist.

"A block of stone is just a block of stone,
And you can tell us of its molecules,
Specific gravity and all the rules
Which make it stay together, but alone,
You must admit it is a block of stone.
But wait, a first appearance often fools
A rash, unwary judge who ridicules
A good opinion that is not his own.
For sculptors, such as Pheidias, would dream
A human figure in his mind and then
Create a likeness from the mass; profound
Resemblance to his prior thought would seem
To prove the value of Ideas, and when
You need examples, simply look around."

And so I did, and all around I saw
(Perhaps I only thought that I had seen)
The glory of the Grecian art, the clean,
Athletic human forms without a flaw,
Appearing perfect and inspiring awe,
Some clothed and others nude (but not obscene),
Surrounding the Academy, between
Ourselves and Athens' plaza, Agora.
The winding path up to Acropolis
Was lined with statues and with temples where
The Victories all stood in echelon;
And at the summit was the edifice
Above all others and beyond compare,
The temple to Athena, Parthenon.

"I think that you can see," the Master said,
"That beauty is around you, everywhere;
You praise the marble statue, but beware,
Ignore the stone and love the form instead,
For mud or wax might have contributed
As much as marble to the image there.
The gross material cannot compare
In value to the dream inherited.
The origin of beauty is the mind,
Abstract creation is the prime event,
And all else follows; perfect execution
Of concepts will impress on undefined
Material, inert recipient,
The image for a perfect resolution."

"The whole of Nature which our senses show,
Depends upon Ideas for its existence;
Material is needed for assistance,
But ideal figures, like an embryo,
Are destined to be born, and live and grow,
Impressing passive things without resistance.
Ideas create our world, but at a distance,
Determining the shape of all we know.
There was an architect, the 'Demiurge',
That brought the matter and the form together
Just as the sculptor brings his ideal dream
To marble, and a statue will emerge.
The forms are perfect and unchanging, whether
The world is flawed, however it might seem."

Now when the sound and babble had subsided,
(Since all the students clamored to agree
And many spoke at once), he looked at me.
"It was our guest," he said, "who has provided
Our topic for discussion, and confided:
With all his knowledge of the galaxy
And sub-atomic force, and gravity,
On 'how to live,' he still is undecided.
For are we destined simply to exist
Within the laws of physics he has shown,
Obeying boundaries that limit action
Like nothing nobler than an atomist?
And do we have volition of our own?
From whence will come our greatest satisfaction?"

I then admitted that I did not know
With all my learning, how to correlate
The proven laws of physics to create
A system for a moral life, although
I knew that it was not the status quo.
For it was Socrates who would debate
Eternally upon the consummate
Perfection the examined life would show.
And so I gladly gave him my permission
To lecture freely on morality,
And even to provide a catechism.
Then he agreed, "You've heard my definition
Of global Beauty and Humanity,
So let us now extend our syllogism."

"A single act of kindness, often brief,
Exists for just a moment, then is gone,
Its essence cast into oblivion
And lost forever; time is like a thief,
Converting momentary joy to grief.
A certain sadness in comparison
To brief but honest pleasure when begun,
Prevents a constant comforting motif.
But memory, a function of the mind,
Can draw together singular events
Into a seamless smooth continuum,
And make of varied virtues one defined
As representing true benevolence,
Thus clarifying each residuum."

"And if our mind can do this on one plane,
Consider what a greater mind might do,
A Universal Reason, one that knew
The purity perfection could attain.
This Mind would create principles, ordain
Eternal true reality, and through
This pattern stamped on human residue,
Create a novel virtuous domain.
Then those enlightened could participate,
And join their actions to the main example:
The constant principle that never changes,
Is rational and always temperate;
Though rigid in its standards, it has ample
Resilience within its stated ranges."

"Then how can someone in this universe
Of shifting shadows of reality
Determine how to live, judiciously
Decide between the better and the worse,
The good and evil acts that intersperse
Throughout our lives, the truth from fallacy
And orthodox belief from heresy?
True choices bring a blessing, false, a curse.
Because our senses are so limited,
Events and single objects transitory,
The world itself presents such obstacles
That, to be valid, truth is based instead
On reason, and determined 'a priori'
On universal, lasting principles."

"Then man must concentrate, and recognize
Ideas and principles that lead to good.
Reliance on desire and pleasure could
Distract the active mind, that otherwise
Would use the energy to analyze
Those varied factors that in likelihood
Might create virtue, those that always should
Be followed purely, with no compromise.
And furthermore, the '*will*' must be controlled;
Unregulated action, courage, bravery,
Without the constant rule of reason must
Lead on to tragedy a hundred-fold,
Like foolish sacrifice, and death and slavery,
And in the eyes of others, deep distrust.

"The goal of life is to release the soul
From bondage to the body, to desire,
To passions and emotions, the entire
Kaleidoscope of things that take their toll.
Without these handicaps, it then is whole
And able to suppress, reject the prior
Existence in exchange for one much higher,
A life of wisdom, courage, self-control.
And this will make one happy, not with pleasure,
But with contentment, when one has achieved
A harmony with all the gods, the Good,
The Demiurge (the Architect), the measure
Of true and perfect Reason, which conceived
The purest status that one ever could."

"The prison of your soul, the physical
Appearance you have known must be denied;
The chaos of sensations that misguide
Your course in life is diametrical
In opposition to the natural
Direction that your reason can provide.
So let your passions go ungratified,
The benefits are unequivocal.
And if you now are ready to deny
The life that you have known, reject and ban
All thoughts of common paths where humans plod,
Lift up your heart and mind, resolve to fly
Away from earth as quickly as you can;
To fly away is to become like God."

I listened carefully to keep abreast
Of all the many thoughts that he presented,
And some seemed true, with others I dissented,
And some I dimly understood at best.
The audience was gracious to its guest
And throughout all this long unprecedented
Extended speech seemed fairly well-contented;
But then I sensed a shift in interest.
The School began to feel a new imperative,
Lost focus on the Master's conversation
With me, this philosophical beginner.
Now exercising their unique prerogative
As students paying for their education,
They rose, dispersed, and went straight home for dinner.

But after their departure, one remained.
He came across the now-deserted space
To meet me, with a rough provincial grace
And accent, one that he had surely gained
Quite early in his life, and still retained
Despite the cultured language of this place.
He carried traits that he could not erase,
A blunt directness which the rest disdained;
For though he was much younger than the Master,
He was not reticent with his ambition,
And often he forgot to be polite.
He contradicted firmly, speaking faster,
Until he sometimes passed that fixed position
Appropriate for such an acolyte.

The younger man admitted this to me:
"I have not always been the best of sons,
Or to my father in philosophy.
There are in legend some comparisons;
When Oedipus had killed old Laius, this
Unconscious act had made available
Jocasta, bringing down the edifice,
The walls that had been unassailable.
My mentor now is old, his time is spent,
And mine is coming, in the interim
I do anticipate some discontent;
The search for wisdom will not die with him,
And though I love his grace, his master's touch,
I truly do not like him very much."

THE LYCEUM

"The prize, philosophy, is there to seize,
And I intend to grasp it if I can.
It was some years ago that I began
To study at the school of Socrates,
Now labeled 'the Academy' where these
Young Greeks despise a Macedonian
By calling me a crude barbarian,
For none of us have ancient pedigrees.
These foppish parasites who gather daily
To listen to the Master, and agree
With any theory that he proposes
Will dance around analyses as gaily
As ribbons on their robes, complacently
Accepting anything that he discloses."

"He has constructed here his edifice
On weak foundations, I myself believe.
Pure reasoning can easily deceive,
And then descend into mere artifice,
If there is not an equal emphasis
On data that we only can achieve
Through observation; otherwise, naïve
And weak are walls of his acropolis.
Like Socrates suspended in his basket
Within the play by Aristophanes,
He is not grounded, has no place to stand;
Between the earth and heaven in his casket
He is afflicted with 'Academese',
Philosopher of all cloud-cuckoo-land."

"For only by an honest argument
And disagreement taken graciously
Can reason conquer gross stupidity.
A tough and rigid logic in dissent
Should not be taken as impertinent,
For I believe in what I hear and see
As well as what I think; that truth must be
A synthesis of these is evident.
He is a poet and a visionary,
And I an honest thinker and logician.
He loves to sit and fantasize, while talking
Of perfect concepts, all imaginary.
I see the world as real, and in addition,
I would myself prefer to think while walking."

"I have been criticized for my collection
Of manuscripts, the knowledge of the past;
But I believe that wisdom, once amassed
Must be protected, serve as a connection
To present thought, and indicate direction
Of research and inquiry to the vast
Unknown before us, and an unsurpassed
Control on philosophical reflection.
I have been called 'the worm of books', whatever
That name might mean; with no apology,
I read and classify and reason more
Than any of the dreamers, or the clever
Debaters and the Sophists, certainly
Beyond those here or any heretofore."

"Enough complaint, I still do love the man,
The teacher, mentor, gracious host and friend;
And for a youth, I could not recommend
A finer guide than this Utopian.
But I have studied with him for a span
Of twenty years, and now do not intend
To stay much longer; all good things will end,
And I will go, politely if I can.
So come, and let us leave this tired museum,
For certainly, your scientific knowledge
Will fit my school. Together we will walk
The path of the gymnasium, Lyceum,
Perhaps attracting others to this college
Who wish to listen as we think and talk."

He took me by the arm, and thus we went
To stroll upon a running-track nearby,
And while we walked he tried to modify
The tirade I had heard, his discontent
With Academic teaching, his dissent,
And grandiose ambition. My reply
Was lost amid torrential speech whereby
He tried to clarify just what he meant.
"Unlike what you might think, I'm not opposed
To one particular philosophy;
For I have read the books, the usual
Long manuscripts of thinkers who disclosed
Confusion, error, and absurdity.
I think they're wrong and foolish, one and all."

"I paid attention while you were explaining
The theses of your modern physicists.
Democritus and all the Atomists
Invoked a system in our time containing
These units, all alike, which while maintaining
A constant motion joined (unless they missed),
To form a complex substance which exists
In combinations, always wax-and-waning.
These atoms mingled, fused and separated
By chance, but were eternal, never changing,
Without a catalyst or master plan.
So Fortune was the factor that dictated
The patterns for these atoms' rearranging,
Producing earthly substances, like man."

"And then there was a natural reaction
Opposing such a mechanistic scheme;
Ideas supplanted atoms as supreme,
Reality was focused on abstraction.
But now this novel philosophic faction
Has gone too far, their system is extreme,
Their perfect forms exist as in a dream
Where proven facts are only a distraction.
The universe, quite immaterial,
Becomes a realm of ideal forms, unchanging,
Eternal uncreated patterns which
Assume fantastic and ethereal
Dim essences that float through space, arranging
Themselves, each one into its proper niche."

"We must come back to earth; a synthesis
Is needed now, between these opposites.
The world we see is real, and thus it fits
What you have said; but my analysis
Reveals that there is even more than this.
An acorn is a solid thing that sits
With weight upon your hand, and this is its
Stability which no one can dismiss.
But much potential lies within this seed,
It will transform itself into a tree.
The tree is its ideal, and not abstract,
But innate in the nut, and guaranteed
To grow into the final form we see;
This transformation is a proven fact."

"There is a form within each block of stone
Which liberated, proves a perfect one.
There may be others too, comparison
Will demonstrate their flaws; this one alone
Is trapped within the marble, still unknown.
The carving, which if carefully begun
Will free the figure, and when all is done
May demonstrate perfection of its own."
I did not say that I already knew
Of one great sculptor and his work, much later,
(Just half of one millennium ago),
Who saw a body trapped in stone, and who
Forever thought himself a liberator
Of youthful David, Michelangelo.

"So form and matter are not separate,
But unified; within each living thing
Resides a soul, each one embodying
A function or a future that as yet
May be invisible, do not forget:
The smallest acorn has the power to spring
Into a tree, its soul determining
The only final form it will beget.
Beginning with this simple model plant,
Progressing upward to a higher being,
The soul of any animal, complex
And multifaceted has elegant
Developmental powers, thus foreseeing
Its needs, like safety, shelter, food and sex."

"But man is on an even higher plane,
His soul is capable of abstract thought,
(Not only what he *does* but what he *ought*),
Enabling him to judge and ascertain
Those tempting things from which he must abstain.
The analytic *reason* man has sought
Has been a blessing, but has also brought
The moral standards which he must maintain.
This reason, as a whole, can be divided
Into a lower, simpler kind, the 'passive',
Intelligent but never innovative,
Inert and ineffective, undecided,
Until its activation by a massive
Infusion by the higher form, 'creative'."

"*Inventive* reason, so unique to man,
Existed prior to the soul's creation,
And will continue after all cessation
Of life within the body. It began
As one divine and simple spark, which can
Invade the body and the soul; formation
Within this unity brings activation
Of what was just utilitarian.
And out of passive possibility
Develops active thought, and this is dual,
Both real and abstract, for analysis
Of man and God (with all humility),
Of life and death and possible renewal,
Of Virtue, Good, and its antithesis."

"Creative force is immaterial,
A gift of God or of divinity,
Belonging to us temporarily,
Infused into the soul, ethereal
(Unlike the passive reason), mystical.
For when the body will have ceased to be,
The lower soul (intelligence), not free,
Will also die, without residual.
But now creative reason, cast adrift,
Will float through space, and finally will earn
Re-entry to the source whence it had come.
So God reclaims his pure and sacred gift,
And though the body dies, with no return,
The world is still in equilibrium."

"My colleague, Plato, sought to make men good,
Believing virtue would cause happiness,
The pleasures of the senses bringing less
Than reason and restraint and wisdom could.
But I have questioned if he understood
To what extent denial creates stress,
How difficult is virtue in excess;
Perfection here, what is the likelihood?
I advocate a life in harmony,
Of moderation, of a 'golden mean',
Still governed by the rules of common sense,
Midway between extremes; serenity
Now seems to me to be the path between
An emptiness and moral turbulence."

"God's gift to me is rationality,
For reason is the final activation
Of God's ongoing process of creation,
The very basis of philosophy,
The source of all of life's true harmony.
How should our lives fit into this equation?
The answer is in constant moderation,
With balance and control and symmetry.
So courage is preferred to cowardice
But also to a rash foolhardiness.
Thus all within your life should be serene,
And ruled by rational analysis,
(Where feelings and desires are powerless)
Within the limits of this golden mean."

I asked him if he could elaborate,
Perhaps define this Virtue as a mean
Between two vices, each of which was seen
By all as equally unfortunate.
He said that modest pride was such a state
To be desired, existing in between
Humility and vanity, routine
Examples that he could enumerate.
Between a prodigality and meanness
Lies generosity, and likewise wit
Is neither a buffoonery nor boorish.
You need not be a slave to excess cleanness,
Nor slovenly; a lover must submit
To neither wildness, nor be amateurish.

Concerning man's essential decency,
I asked if middling truthfulness was good,
And was integrity misunderstood
Since all equate it with philosophy.
He said that boasting or false modesty
(Applied to one's own inner self), both could
Be taken as an arrogance, and should
Be buffered with sincere apology.
But abstract honesty is not a mean,
True justice cannot be negotiated,
 For these are virtues that seem absolutes;
A person who aspires to be serene
And well-respected must have advocated
In their entirety these attributes.

Then I became the Devil's Advocate
And asked if Virtue would stay virtuous
If it were more than average, and thus
Exceeded what he said the golden state,
The mean, the compromise would tolerate.
Was there some limit, some mysterious
Extent of goodness, some fortuitous
Locale where Good and Bad dissociate?
If more than common virtue is destructive,
And less is more, so we should there withdraw,
Be satisfied with moderate endeavor,
With lives both ordinary and productive,
Forget about the glory and the awe
Of God's own kingdom, settle for "whatever".

"Not quite", he said, "The mean does not apply
To contemplation by the intellect,
Which is the best of all you can effect.
Since virtue is the way to gratify
Man's need for happiness, then this is why
There is no limit to the mind's correct
Endeavors; justice, virtue, both reflect
(Along with honesty) on those who try.
The highest good of man, to realize
His reason as completely as he can
Brings happiness and pleasure, harmony.
When ordinary virtues synchronize,
Controlled by reason, balanced, such a man
Of his free will achieves divinity."

Throughout his thinking there were imperfections,
And some were major, some to him unique,
(The strong and wise important, not the weak);
To slavery he had no real objections,
And this was so for slaves of all complexions
As long as they did not include a Greek.
His attitude toward evil was oblique,
An absence of the good, or mis-directions.
He had a personal indifference
To suffering (except among his friends),
And human misery was quite abstract.
Within his system true benevolence,
Unselfishness or sympathy extends
No further than analysis, in fact.

There was a poverty of real emotion
Throughout his arguments, and no compassion.
He seemed detached, objective, with devotion
Reserved for theory, and in this fashion
Appeared to be both comfortable and smug
While speaking to his peers, philosophers,
Reserving for the moral life a shrug,
Dismissing what a common man incurs.
He felt the best of men should have great pride,
And looked upon humility as vice;
The poor and humble were unqualified
To even dream of earthly paradise.
Throughout his teachings, I found nothing there
To comfort one in need, or in despair.

Thus, in the end I did not join his school,
Although I walked with him around his track,
Lyceum, and could never over-rule
His reasoning, but still there was a lack
Of what I needed in my life; he spoke
To men of comfort, but with little need,
To those in power, but who never woke
In fear, without salvation guaranteed.
He never had a deep experience
Of love or loss, of death or ecstasy;
Despite integrity and eloquence
He could not adequately speak to me.
And so I left him, and went on alone,
From pagan times into the great unknown.

THE CITY OF GOD

The shining city crested on a hill
And there the ancient Roman road ran near;
It was in disrepair, its engineer
No longer cared, perhaps had lost his skill.
Between the road and city, there was still
A reconstructed Roman bath, austere
But still intact; a monastery here
Had bent a pagan building to its will.
I had a need that I should solve somehow,
And so I left the major road, and there
An ancient monk approached along the path.
"Our august bishop will receive you now."
I did not welcome sermons or a prayer,
When all I really wanted was a bath.

The bishop was a small and scrawny man
Appearing like an animated bird,
And simply clothed, as if he'd never heard
That bishops dress as richly as they can
(But plainer than a pope); no better than
A humble servant was what he preferred.
This unassuming style perhaps occurred
From little contact with the Vatican.
He lived in study, poverty and prayer,
Establishing a strong and strict tradition
Of closed monastic living, also greatly
Defining Christian doctrine everywhere.
He was a saint, and of his own volition
Was celibate as well, but only lately.

I heard he was dogmatic, this was true,
And as a person, sensitive as well.
He could define the boundaries of hell,
And faced with paradox, could still pursue
A single minded argument, and due
To primal faith, he often could compel
Capitulation of an infidel
Or heretic whom he might interview.
But like a lot of latter-day conversions,
He was quite touchy on the subject of
His life before the light of inspiration.
He felt to mention this would cast aspersions
Upon himself; he could not rise above
This issue, which remained an aggravation.

At odds with St.Jerome, who was his friend,
Donatus who was not, and Eutyches,
He fought the Manicheans, heresies
Like that of Arius who would amend
The nature of his Lord and try to bend
The orthodox toward ambiguities;
(He preached until a violent disease
Revealed his human weakness in the end).
The Christians found, in councils like Nicaea,
The bishop was correct, the others null,
Declaring their opinions to be void.
This vindication was no panacea,
Despite his theologic pinnacle
The controversies left him paranoid.

This I observed when he addressed me thus:
"I see that you attended seminary,
Or spent some time within a monastery;
Your spirit seems to be ambiguous,
A little learning, not conspicuous,
But just enough to be seditionary,
A grating gadfly of an adversary,
With arguments I'll prove erroneous.
I'll wager that you know the silly ditty
Concerning me, passed down by seminarians
For centuries, and quoted when excited
Or tipsy students want to prove they're witty;
They test my patience like the Unitarians."
And then, without my asking, he recited:

"Of all the men I've ever known,
Whether saints or on a throne,
Each had his sins and minor faults,
A few spare bones in closets and vaults.
Some reformed and some did not,
(Some like it cool, some like it hot)."

"Morals were in a complete upheaval
As traffic was heavy 'twixt good and evil.
Of all these men who went between,
The smartest by far was Augustine.
He had his fun and then repented,
Surviving the mess quite lilac-scented."

"He split his life as with a rod,
'Half for me, and half for God.'
But *his* half first he shrewdly spent
On women, wine, and merriment.
He got himself to a state so lowly,
It took a while to make him holy."

"But when the Church became acquainted
With this conversion, it had him sainted.
He wrote of Rome and Roman sin,
The trouble that pleasure will get you in;
So take his advice, and never be bad,
Don't think of the fun St. A. must have had."

"Oh, slander, sacrilege and heresy",
He cried to me, "although I must admit,
There is a fair amount of truth in it;
It should have been more complimentary.
It has bad rhythm and no simile
Or metaphor, and though the requisite
Poor rhymes are there, it has but little wit,
And borders on a rank apostasy.
Do you agree, sir, that you heard this verse
In school, in classes in philosophy,
And sang it later, with a beer or two,
Then passed it on to others, even worse,
You may have written it yourself; feel free
To take whatever credit that is due."

But I protested, I had never heard
These verses, never been to seminary,
Did not intend to be an adversary,
And thought the whole affair was quite absurd.
Surprisingly, he all at once concurred,
"Then you must pardon my imaginary
Suspicions, these are always temporary,
I happily confess when I have erred."
And then he seemed completely to forget
Our nervous and excited introduction.
He brought me to his son, Adeodatus,
His "gift of God", a recent epithet,
Replacing "son of sin", a past construction,
Conceding both reflected on his status.

He looked me over carefully, then blurted,
"I know where you have been, what did you seek
Among philosophers? Are you a Greek?
And are you still a pagan, or converted?"
This sudden challenge left me disconcerted,
Unready to respond, except to speak
In phrases disconnected and oblique,
With reassurances that I inserted.
I was a seeker of enlightenment,
But at this time did not require conversion.
The small philosophy I had acquired
Left ample space for any subsequent
Illumination I could find; immersion
Within his thoughts was what I now desired.

With this disclaimer, he seemed satisfied
And did not press for any true credential,
Accepting me as showing some potential
For learning, with a mind unoccupied
With prejudice, a slate with one blank side.
I must have seemed to him the quintessential
Fresh candidate to combat existential
Philosophy of Plato. He replied,
"Since you have had such trouble finding me,
And say you wish to learn what I can teach,
Then I will show you how I found the border
Between our faith and Greek philosophy,
And merged the two, thus justifying each;
And so creating, out of chaos, order."

"You know that I inherited a mess,
And one not suited for the shallow-hearted;
For centuries ago, our Lord departed,
And left behind confusion and distress.
His followers had faith, but less success
Interpreting the complex course He charted.
It is a wonder that the church got started,
The pit of problems almost bottomless.
Just one at first: describe the Christian God
And say exactly how he might align
With views of Aristotle, those of Plato,
And Evil in the universe (quite odd
But true), no end of trouble to define;
They handed me this rather warm potato."

"So I began with Plato's Demiurge,
A sort of architect, which first I used;
I clarified the concept, and infused
Some goodness, wisdom, love, began to merge
Pure reason to the mixture, and diverge
From pagan limitation, and excused
Those ancient features which were most confused,
And slowly saw the Christian God emerge.
And pagan Evil, I re-named as Sin,
Defining this by Adam's deviation
From purest harmony with God's perfection
To arrogance that had its origin
In momentary sexual temptation,
Resulting in a moral insurrection."

"This allegory is recorded in
The Jewish Bible, and the Christian version;
Then came Vespasian and the Great Dispersion
And nothing was the same as it had been.
The rabbis' and the scholars' discipline
Was broken and diluted; with conversion
Some brought with them, along with their immersion,
Their ancient Jewish principles of sin.
But others, Greeks and pagans were converted
To add philosophy to our equation,
And, to be honest, this had anteceded
By centuries what now our Church asserted,
That God had sent a single revelation;
To cool this cauldron, sorcerers were needed."

"Apparently, the early bishops thought
I was a theological magician,
And honestly, I did have some ambition;
If it were possible, I felt I ought
To organize their currently distraught
Confused and somewhat mystical position,
And reconcile our faith with Greek tradition,
To justify those things our Master taught.
And maybe they had also read 'Confessions',
A work that I had written honestly,
Relating to my uncommitted youth.
Admitting to some early indiscretions,
I then discovered in austerity
A long and winding pathway to the truth."

"They left me many issues, ill-defined,
The most important was the Trinity,
A new and complex God, a deity
That must replace all pagan gods combined.
And how is God related to mankind?
What is the nature of humanity?
And is obedience compulsory?
These were among the answers I must find.
But first, before beginning this great mission,
One crucial problem needs considering:
True knowledge is a slippery thing when new,
But hardens over time, in this condition
Becoming basic for our reasoning;
How do we know that what we know is true?"

"A stream of knowledge flows into the mind,
It may be true or may be just illusion,
May clarify our thoughts or cause confusion,
Some parts specific, others undefined,
And we must ascertain the valid kind.
Within the world, there is a vast profusion
Of teachers who rely on self-delusion.
I'll give you two examples, intertwined:
First, Plato tried to show that pure conception
Of mental images (Ideas) was real,
But this relied on human intellect.
Then Aristotle focused on perception,
What sensory awareness could reveal,
But this again to me seemed incorrect."

"They asked me to resolve the Trinity,
Deciding who was who and what was what,
And what was made, and who was unbegot.
For everybody knew that there were three
Distinctive features of our deity,
Three facets; though a Unity cannot
Divide itself, perhaps it can allot
Its attributes to work in harmony.
So I agreed with Athanasius
Against the many current heretics
Who fiddled with this problem, disagreed
Among themselves and were oblivious
To all imperatives of politics,
Where unity is needed to succeed."

"The same applies to all things orthodox,
Simplicity and concentration are
Advantages compared to similar
But more diffuse constructions; stumbling-blocks
Will disappear if clarity unlocks
An understanding, in particular
The Gnostic inspiration was bizarre,
They never understood this paradox.
Theology must always organize,
And so must all of our authority;
Commandments from above, to be obeyed,
Must have divine imprimatur, arise
From Holy Scripture, or the papacy,
The stamp of long tradition overlaid."

"Religious truth, not always logical,
Escapes a rigorous analysis;
To build a theologic edifice
One needs a base that's more than scriptural.
But no one can rely on personal
Perception or his own hypothesis
Initiated in the mind, for this
Will often prove to be irrational.
So in the greater matter of salvation,
And in the fate of man's immortal soul,
In order to avoid heresy
There is a need of sacred revelation
That leads to true belief, and on the whole,
I trust the truth that God reveals to me."

"First, God is good (and this is absolute
By any theologic definition),
Creating everything by his volition,
The Matter, Forms, Ideas that constitute
The Grecian universe, and each minute
Electron that is in the world; this mission,
Spontaneous, complete, without transition,
Came from the Mind of God, without dispute.
Before this moment (which was unassisted),
There was no thing created or destroyed,
And in addition, this event took place
Before our time began, for God existed
Alone and in a dark and boundless void;
For also, He created time and space."

"Thus all that was, or is, or ever will
Exist within the world is a creation
Of God, and seeks its perfect consummation
Returning to its source; yet to fulfill
Its destined role within the world, until
It can achieve its final revelation,
It tries to close its present separation
By reaching through the space remaining still.
But what could make this process difficult?
Impulses such as love are all divine,
Beginning in the Mind of God, and yes,
Within a perfect world the one result
Would be that all created things align
Into the Will of God, and righteousness."

"The problem here is fairly obvious
(My answer is a little complicated),
For looking at the world that God created,
It seems to be somewhat ambiguous.
If it was made so well, a curious
Inconstancy is often demonstrated,
A feature He had not anticipated:
The world is not completely virtuous.
And you might wonder, quite respectfully,
Since God is power, knowledge, all that's good,
And would not tolerate a deviation
From His divine intent, how can this be,
That things occurred, not really as they should?
I worked the answer out: predestination."

"Since God not only was all-powerful,
But knew exactly all that He was doing,
Then, following Creation, His ensuing
Dissatisfaction was predictable.
For He is always able to annul
These ancient vices which are ever brewing,
And new ones also, that we keep accruing;
It only needs a minor miracle.
By definition, God is not surprised
At what occurs within the world He made,
Or with the faults and frailties of man.
Nor does He think His project ill-advised,
For even after Adam's escapade,
It all is still consistent with His plan."

"As darkness is an absence of the light,
Thus Evil is comparable to Good;
And God created both, so contrast would
Illuminate His glory in our sight.
And if these opposites can re-unite,
His virtue will prevail and, understood
Correctly, make us live just as we should;
So does a beacon guide us through the night.
The light itself cannot be overcome,
And even though the darkness might surround
The single focus of illumination,
Its presence gives us equilibrium,
And all within its range will sense profound
Relief and confidence and validation."

"And then, I tackled Sin, its definition.
Now, anyone can say that it exists,
Especially that person who resists
Reluctantly (myself); is this condition
Consistent with an innocent omission?
Or is a conscious action that persists
Required for sin? And what if one assists
A sinner, Would this justify perdition?
I reconstructed all that might displease
And analyzed the actions of the actors,
Comparing motives, trying thus to measure
Small misdemeanors versus felonies,
And in this way determining which factors
Would bypass or might merit God's displeasure."

"The snake was evil, Eve accommodating,
And Adam chose the path that led to sin.
For having rights of first refusal in
Those matters of temptation, he kept hating
The thought of missing pleasure, alternating
With equal fear of God's strict discipline;
And yet seduction of the feminine
And its charisma left him vacillating.
But to each person there will come a time
When he must make an affirmation or
A grand rejection, no hypocrisy;
Then saying 'Yes' will make his life sublime,
The 'No', the destined 'No' we all abhor
Will crush his life throughout eternity."

"So with the first and last of man's free will,
Adam chose, and kept the love of Eve,
But lost the confidence of God; naïve
And foolish as this was, perhaps he still
Retained illusions of a codicil
To God's divine agreement, which would leave
To him his earthly pleasure, and retrieve
His soul's salvation, due to God's goodwill.
Or did he think that God would just forget
His contract with His ultimate creation?
Or maybe second chances were permitted,
A short detour; he might/might not *regret*,
But with some pleas and proper adoration
Would be forgiven or perhaps acquitted."

"But Adam truly underestimated
The gravity of his new situation,
For God was serious about creation,
And knowing all, He had anticipated
That man's perfection might be over-rated,
Thus causing him to try a declaration
Of independence and emancipation;
And His suspicions now were vindicated.
For God gave Man one chance, and one chance only,
Demanding good behavior in exchange
For Life, and being somewhat over-nice,
Anticipated that he might be lonely;
So God was even gracious to arrange
A comrade for his time in paradise."

"While having all these various illusions
Of how their disobedience might end,
Their fantasies (that God would condescend
To offer them a series of exclusions
From His authority), were mere delusions.
The Law was *firm,* and God did not amend
The standards of obedience, or bend
The rules to create happier conclusions.
So when they left their paradise, while packing,
Could they be angry, were they merely sad?
The snake had never told them of the rumor:
There was one thing that God Himself was lacking,
In spite of all His power and love He had
A very undeveloped sense of humor."

"As Adam ate the apple that he craved
(And Eve had made available), the sin
Of disobedience now entered in,
Along with knowledge; they had misbehaved.
The road to Hell is elegantly paved,
Not only for those two; the origin,
The seed of all to come, to our chagrin,
Contains this primal fault, and none are saved.
Or none, that is, without the special grace
That God bestows on some; just as a prism
Makes colors out of light, so separation
Of saved (elect) from damned is commonplace
Within the Mind of God (but first, baptism
Would be required), and thus, predestination."

The basis of his complex argument
He found within the writings of St. Paul,
The letter to the Romans, over all,
Which he expanded to a great extent.
He took those parts he found convenient,
And did not hesitate to overhaul
Some texts and implications to forestall
Objections and corrections and dissent.
"We go to heaven not because we're good,
For all of us are totally depraved,
But strictly due to God's unending grace.
No reason can be given why one should
Be saved and others not, the well-behaved
May also end in some disgraceful place."

I thought perhaps that I misunderstood,
But he insisted that divine damnation
Was due to God's great justice, and salvation
A product of his mercy, both were good
In equal measure; therefore we all should
Be grateful for this (fateful) revelation,
And hope for His benign adjudication
While here on earth, and do the best we could.
His logic showed a perfect prejudice,
He reasoned backward, with a rigid mind;
He knew the answer, then made up the question.
But with his theologic synthesis
Of pagan thought and Godly Truth combined,
He almost proved that Plato was a Christian.

With this, I knew that I was lost, for he
Was more persuasive, more aggressive than
The usual religious partisan,
A dominating personality.
Within my mind, I thought I could foresee
Surrender to a moral superman,
For he proclaimed himself custodian
Of Holy Truth, and I was only me.
I recognized that he, obsessed with sin,
Was blind to love and beauty in our lives;
His grim, forbidding vision might be true,
But I could not accept as genuine
A universe or God who thus deprives
Us of His love, and hope of heaven, too.

He offered me salvation if I could
Renounce my present life and earthly sin,
Exchange the body's pleasure for the good
Of penance, prayer and moral discipline.
The key to my redemption was denial,
Assuring heaven; in the interim,
He offered me a temporary trial
If I would join his order, live like him.
I liked austerity in hypothetic
But not in personal and harsh conditions,
And though his life was stark and quite ascetic
His mind was not so pure, he had ambitions;
I sensed a devious and deeper goal,
And saw that he was coveting my soul.

But I myself could barely understand
His explanation of the mysteries;
And all his elegant analyses
Depended first on faith, and then on grand
Subjective logic, which however planned,
Was less than Aristotle's *unities,*
Denying obvious realities
That I could see and hear and touch first-hand.
He was sincere and earnest and was set,
Maintaining that the extra-ordinary
Complexities of faith were real, and yet
Although I tried, it would not come to me.
I left him in his monastery, still
Beneath the shining city on the hill.

THE ANGELIC DOCTOR

The Church for over seven hundred years,
With thinkers such as Peter Abelard,
And Roscelin and Anselm, St. Bernard,
And Erigena (churchmen whose careers
Fell short of recognizing new frontiers),
Repressed or hindered any avant-garde
Conceptions which the Pope would disregard;
Creative thought completely disappears.
But there was one who formed a synthesis
Of all this rather modest variation
Of Christian doctrine, his revisionary
Achievement built a lasting edifice
Significant today. By chance location,
My path ran close beside his monastery.

The monk was both a large and heavy man,
But quiet and content to learn and teach,
More calm and modest, courteous with each
Disciple, student, adversary than
His colleagues since the early Church began.
In patient conversation, prudent speech,
His style was Rational, thus he would preach,
Unlike St. Augustine's Utopian.
His native northern German heritage
Of reason, logic, not of histrionic
Ecstatic inspiration meant that he
Endured the disconcerting privilege
Of being called (although he was Teutonic)
By some, "The great dumb ox of Italy".

And therefore, I was not surprised to find
That he was gracious as he welcomed me,
And that he made a place where we could be
Relaxed, and in a fellowship defined
As students, pilgrims, residents combined
With those who taught, a "goodly company",
Who sought to show, with skill and piety,
That Aristotle was with Christ aligned.
Not only did he give the pagans credit,
But Avicenna and Maimonides,
And Isaac the Israeli, Abelard,
And also al-Ghazali, sought to edit
Albertus Magnus, whose analyses
Were at the time considered avant-garde.

And that is how I found myself to be
Again involved within a group that learned
By free discussion, largely unconcerned
By rank or status; this equality
Seemed due to universal piety.
Thus, one unique occurrence I discerned:
When time for mass or vespers, they adjourned,
Unlike Lyceum or Academy.
But I was on the edges, on the borders
Of this group also, though they were Scholastic,
And I was somewhat of a learned man;
I had not taken any holy orders,
The central figures there were all monastic,
And many, like the saint, Dominican.

Observing interactions in this group
I saw that it was far from being Greek;
Democracy has always been unique,
A freely thinking and unbiased troop
Of equals, no one needing to recoup
Misplaced authority with double-speak,
And no one fearing personal critique
Like being called an utter nincompoop.
But here the obvious authority
Prevailed because of thorough, deeper learning;
Despite the silly name I heard him called,
He knew his Greek, he knew philosophy,
He knew his Aristotle, overturning
Those heresies of which he was appalled.

But mainly they agreed, as Realists,
That universals had reality,
And sought examples for analogy,
Researching essences as scientists,
Or more specifically, biologists,
To prove without a doubt ascendancy
Of God's creation, which continually
Produces things of which the world consists.
Thus they denied creation as a single
Unique event that never was repeated,
Maintaining that we always are surrounded
By substances and matter which commingle
Until their formal union is completed
And yet another creature is compounded.

The monks believed in reason over all
(But not above their loyalty to Christ),
And none would willingly have sacrificed
The doctrines of the Church, should this befall:
That conflict proved a need to overhaul
The older *Truth Revealed*, which had sufficed
For centuries, for *Reasoned Truth*, enticed
From pagans by historical recall.
The Saint himself, Aquinas, knew that trees
Could differ in their leaves, their bark, their height,
But unified in "treeness" were unique.
These universal qualities were keys
Consolidating essences despite
The differences that scientists might seek.

A *universal* was a catalyst
That acted on a substrate he called "matter".
He thought that both the former and the latter
Must have a common source, and co-exist
Together at creation, and consist
Of sturdy syntheses which would not shatter
When called from nothingness, then caused to scatter
Throughout the world by God, Protagonist.
All nature is a union, universal;
Its principles (what makes a tree a tree)
Combine with matter (that which separates
The oaks from elms), occurring in rehearsal
At first within the mind of God, then free
Within the universe that He creates.

And man is universal as "Mankind";
He likewise out of nothing was created,
But does contain a certain allocated
Amount of matter through which God designed
Our bodies, individual, defined
To be unique, and each one designated
To be instilled with some illuminated
Allotment of the Universal Mind.
This obvious duality between
The body (matter) and the spirit (soul)
Is similar in all the universe;
And there are forces there, divine, pristine,
That pull man up to God, while some control
The sin that sits upon us like a curse.

The Master showed that God created man
From nothing into actuality;
But all of us contain an oddity,
(Each Christian, pagan and barbarian,
A princess, lady or a courtesan).
These entities embrace duality,
Both sides a separate modality,
But both united since their lives began.
One element is spirit, mind or soul,
That represents a spark of the divine,
The other, body, sinful and debased.
Thus life, a constant struggle for control,
Must look to God in prayer, and then combine
Humility and efforts to be chaste.

As Augustine brought Plato to theology,
(Eternal visions of divine perfection),
Aquinas advocated one correction,
And added Aristotle's terminology
Of "Unmoved Mover" and his methodology
Of following in retrograde direction
Celestial movement, motion whose projection
Reveals a perfect, sanctified cosmology.
He also traced the graduated scale
From very lowest levels of existence
Through stages toward a higher, better creature,
To human consciousness (still often frail),
That senses sanctity, but at a distance,
Inferring God, with flawlessness His feature.

Then, what to say of immortality,
And its companion concept, resurrection?
The soul of man was added, an injection
Into the body's insufficiency.
The soul is not dependent, truthfully,
Upon the body's life, since its projection
Beyond the time of death, a re-direction,
Exists and functions through eternity.
Since God created every human soul,
(The necessary vital principle
Of body's gross material), it lives
Forever as it did in life; its goal
Is merging into God, its pinnacle,
The ultimate of all imperatives.

A man may choose to act or not to act,
For God creates the human will as free.
Thus we must exercise judiciously
This privilege, and understand the fact
That what we do is done, and not retract
Our purposes; in immaturity
We think that we can change reality
And make the repercussions more abstract.
Intention will not make a bad act good,
But only virtuous intent can make
An action that may have good consequences
Into a blessing; acting as we *should*
(Although it may result in a mistake)
Is one of God's most favored preferences.

So, how would he advise that we should live?
Divinity alone provides salvation;
But even God requires co-operation,
Though He is always willing to forgive,
His mercy generous (but not a sieve),
Allowing freely our determination
To take or to reject the invitation,
Accepting Grace or its alternative.
So, in the matter of our own behavior,
We should renounce our wealth, our worldly goods,
Retire into the moral sanctuary
Provided by the model of our Savior,
Live inwardly, in saintly neighborhoods
Of which the best would be a monastery.

For in this pious setting, I assume,
He would not have to chase a concubine
(Whom he discovered naked and supine
And furnished by his mother), with a broom
Thus sweeping her completely from his room.
He felt compelled to make a holy sign
For many hours, until he felt divine
Forgiveness cancel all his guilt and gloom.
Temptations in this world left him appalled;
He traded them for prayer and contemplation
And sought the Will of God. He was a relic
Of bygone virtue, and, as he was called
(Both as a man and also acclamation
As doctor of theology), "angelic".

For he had nothing but a great contempt
For all this world, the sin and evil in it,
And said we should escape this very minute.
This world was well-designed to test and tempt
The body into acts it never dreamt
Were possible; we should not stay within it,
But seek the realm of God (if we could win it),
Renouncing sin, and from it be exempt.
This life, he said, was but a pilgrimage,
A journey through a swamp of tribulation,
A path by which a man might find escape
From sordid evil life, to disengage
From consequences of his degradation,
And by the Grace of God assume His shape.

His virtues were unique among his peers
(If there were truly any at that time).
He was original, a paradigm,
His intellect the type that perseveres
Through controversies lasting many years,
Achieving syntheses that are sublime,
A major theologian in his prime
Who dominates, but never domineers.
He fought the heretics into defeat,
In all the Church's schisms intervened,
Where never did he lose, concede or yield.
When all the souls on earth were fields of wheat,
And there were golden harvests to be gleaned,
He was a tireless worker in the field.

He was not fully honest when he said
(And some have even called him insincere),
That he would follow reason where it led
No matter if the end-point was unclear;
For his conclusions were already fixed,
Ahead of all his brilliant arguments,
The truth already there, declared, unmixed,
In Church theology and sacraments.
Whenever his philosophy supported
Secure established doctrines, well-and-good,
But inconvenient outcomes were aborted;
Then, "Aristotle was misunderstood".
If reason did not solve a situation,
He (and the Church) could count on revelation.

Despite the lack of open-mindedness,
His reasoning and logic were impressive;
But so were spartan meals and comfortless
Accommodations, clothing, and obsessive
Reliance on their prayers and on devotions.
These both were frequent, lengthy, and I noted
Were long on liturgy, as for emotions,
There was remorse and shame, on which they doted.
He said austerity would compensate
For passion, lust and evil tendencies;
How many cravings could accumulate
When so much time was spent upon one's knees?
But I declined to be that great a sinner,
And did not stay beyond a meager dinner.

RENAISSANCE ETHICS AND POLITICS

Then after I had left the monastery,
I sensed that I was passing a divide,
A fundamental chasm now so wide
That had it been a lake or estuary
One could have crossed it only by a ferry.
And looking backwards from the other side,
I knew philosophy must now decide
If it was to become revisionary.
The synthesis attempted through the years
By pious theologians and Scholastics
With Aristotle's Greek philosophy
Showed contradictions, which had caused some fears
Among the insecure ecclesiastics
That they would be accused of heresy.

Then arching over all the great morass
I saw a bridge, beginning where I stood,
On land that had been certified as good,
With re-inforcement daily in the Mass,
And narrow-minded rules to overpass
Suppressed dissent that might (in likelihood)
Become free thought, and later even could
Create a wide, undisciplined crevasse.
But so it came about, and certitude
Gave way to newly-generated doubt;
The price of progress, and of honest search
In open discourse was severe and rude:
Rejection of unquestioning devout
Obedience to teachings of the Church.

The bridge was narrow, like the Pont des Arts
With alcoves at some intervals, and there
A traveler could turn out, stand and stare;
And if that person had a timid heart
He'd not look down, but backward to the start,
To old foundations, now in disrepair
Which rose from Church authority and prayer,
From revelation, and from faith in part.
Nor would he look ahead to where the bridge
Now ended in a new and open land
Where independent thought, not regulated
Led through chaotic space, up to a ridge
With unimpeded views, where one could stand
And see the world, now unadulterated.

Italians built the bridge, the Florentines
Were first to challenge strict authority
Of priests and monks and popes; theology
Had lost significance as Ghibellines
And then the merchant class developed means
Of taking power, creating tyranny
Built more on riches than philosophy,
Reducing popes to trifling figurines.
This secular and humanistic power
Was earnest in its culture, not its morals,
Nor in an organized religion which
Controlled society, and could devour
A heretic with doubts, resolving quarrels
By *truth revealed*, (while still becoming rich).

But independence and enlightenment,
And freedom from a predetermined plan
(Of rigid thought and doctrine) that began
When first this bridge was crossed, was an event
That could result in much bewilderment.
For opening one's mind and limits can
Be much more insecure and daunting than
A regimen that banishes dissent.
For there is comfort in conformity,
Assurance from without gives inner peace;
If we accept a doctrine without doubt
And live in absolute security,
Then all the chaos of our lives will cease,
We will be as complacent as devout.

So this new class constructed their foundation
Of one great bridge to future modern thought
Upon the discord Aristotle brought
To Christian and Platonic combination;
A synthesis that served, since its creation
A thousand years before, as what was taught,
An autocratic discipline which ought
To be accepted blindly for salvation.
This change of old authority, re-birth,
Depended more on weakness and decline
Of prior orders, which had passed their prime
Than on what new conceptions might be worth.
With all their freedom, no one could define
(Except in politics), a paradigm.

Despite this humanistic activism
While Church authority was disappearing,
No theoretic leader was appearing
Who could define this move to modernism;
For they were more concerned with pragmatism,
With power, politics and engineering.
One man alone observed, not interfering,
His name synonymous with cynicism.
He praised Caesare Borgia for his skill,
His lack of scruples and his cleverness,
Not *having* virtue but for *seeming to*.
Soliciting the Medici's good will
When he was out of favor, in distress,
He tried to tell Lorenzo what he knew.

And as I crossed the bridge he waited there;
In retrospect, he saw the centuries
Of positive assurance, during these,
Morality was absolute, to dare
To offer up a less-than-pious prayer
Would be the worst of improprieties.
But now the Florentines and Genoese
Ignored morality, or did not care.
Now only papal states, to keep their power
Preserved religious forms; all else pretended,
Rejecting faith when that was necessary,
But keeping the appearance in that hour
When all their popular support depended
On virtue, even when imaginary.

He stood within a wayside in the route
Which led across the bridge that far ahead
Would end within a land inhabited
By people who, immensely less devout,
Exchanged new scientific proof for doubt,
Relying on experience instead
Of dogma that they had inherited;
The Church was something they might live without.
And he was something like a premonition,
Of all that was to come, the honesty,
And lack of bias and of prejudice.
His contribution was the abolition
Of wishful thinking and of fantasy,
Creating rational analysis.

This was the man who waited there for me,
His slender figure, pale and narrow face
Enclosed in black, without a single trace
Of cordial feelings or sincerity.
His piercing eyes were dark, suspiciously
Examining myself, the interspace
Between us for a proper starting place
Before proceeding with his theory.
His lips were thin, severe and tightly closed,
A man of constant thought, not one of action;
He showed no spirit visible outside,
Not one component of his soul exposed.
His friends believed his honesty abstraction,
And when he told the truth, they thought he lied.

He knew no metaphysics, little ethics,
Except as servant to his politics.
He knew no Lord, condemned no heretics,
Had no theology and no aesthetics,
Did not believe in free-will or ascetics
Nor atheists, whom he called lunatics
Because they lost the votes of Catholics;
He spoke from knowledge, not from theoretics.
But he profoundly knew of men's behavior,
Exposing clearly their dishonesty,
But never judging this a sin or vice;
For when men need a leader or a savior,
They will embrace an image willingly,
And often mere dissembling will suffice.

He wrote "Ten Books of Livy-the Discourses",
Completing only three, and these in hope
That Alexander VI (who then was Pope)
Might see himself in place within the sources
Of papal power; thus he reinforces
The value of religion, and its scope
As social cement to the State, the soap
That cleanses evil and divisive forces.
Much more agnostic than an atheist,
He cared but little for religious truth;
The Roman gods were equally effective
As Christ or Yahweh, called up to assist
Converting savage anarchistic youth
Into a safe republican collective.

The pope then died, as popes will sometimes do,
And left his son, Caesare, powerless.
The Medici now filled the emptiness
As tyrants, by a military coup.
This ruined Machiavelli, for his new
"Militia" fled in battle; in distress
And left without a patron, or access
To popes (now Medici) he tried anew.
But this was difficult, for in addition
To losing Florence to the Holy League,
He fought against, not with, the Medici.
They were not known to tolerate contrition
In others, in the annals of intrigue
They all rejected such apology.

Yet, changing loyalties again, he tried,
His summarized political equation
Was sent (along with fulsome dedication)
At first to Giuliano; when he died
A copy to Lorenzo, who replied
With silence. Thus the hoped for acclamation
Became instead political castration,
And left him bitter and unsatisfied.
Since he was flattering the tyrants now,
He concentrated on how states were won
(And held and lost), and what was salutary
For rulers to survive: to disavow
Both faith and honor when their work was done,
But take them up again when necessary.

Appearing almost as a puritan,
Severe, emotions consciously withheld,
His attitude reserved and paralleled
By subtlety more calculating than
The ordinary honest person can
Conceive, his image equally repelled
And fascinated; in his hands he held
The symbols of a semi-gentleman.
And these, his gloves, were of the quality
That often would impress a novice or
A servant, who approaching him would sense
The presence of assured authority.
Thus those around him felt inferior,
Impressions that were no coincidence.

He said to me: "Now you have surely met
The only honest man that you will meet.
The rest are filled with dreams or self-deceit,
Delusions which will certainly beget
Fantastic misconceptions and regret
Whenever facts of error or defeat
Are entered on the final balance-sheet;
Reality is fatal to forget.
So I have looked beyond the superficial
To find the basic essence, the foundations
Of all that happens in this world; and you
Must learn to penetrate beyond initial
Impressions and cosmetic alterations
To find the central meaning that is true."

"A prince will perish if he's always good,
A virtue is at times a flaw; a fault
(Such as a lack of faith) can often vault
One man above where other men have stood
On principle, stagnating while they should
Examine worthless pledges and default,
Re-write the rules and make a new assault
More likely to succeed than old ones would.
But one must learn to be a great deceiver,
Dissemble well, pretend to be quite gracious
With skilled deception; even a prodigious
Untruthfulness will find a true believer.
And though in private, he may be salacious
A prince should always seem to be religious."

"All princes and all prophets who are armed
Have conquered; those exposed and weak have failed.
And thus Savonarola was impaled
And burned despite the sermons that had charmed
The mob of Florence, for he had alarmed
The pope, whose pack of 'mad-dogs' then assailed
The monk with greater forces, and prevailed;
By strength and not by virtue he was harmed.
And likewise Brutus, good and honest man,
Had liberated Rome by killing Caesar,
But then in contrast to Mark Antony
He turned himself into an also-ran,
No man of power, but a rank appeaser,
Who abdicated Rome, pathetically."

"In all of Christianity to date
The most essential man (including Christ)
Was no one who at all had sacrificed
His time or soul or life to advocate
This new religion, but the chief of state
Of Rome and of its army, who, enticed
By military victory had priced
Religion equal to an empire's fate.
An emperor created Christ's domain
By force of arms, which is the only way
That prophets ever conquer and prevail.
If Constantine had chosen to abstain,
Perplexed apostles, that confused array,
Would certainly be destined then to fail."

"Before he saw 'in hoc signo vinces',
This Christianity, in disarray,
Seemed merely one of many castaway
Religious sects that had no fixed address,
And little skill in how to coalesce.
Disparate units (which to their dismay
Were just as prone to quarrel as to pray),
Had taken independence to excess.
They spent their secret time together huddled
In public buildings or in private homes,
Their ritual resembling rough rehearsal.
Disciples and apostles seemed befuddled
So they could make, confined to catacombs,
No progress toward becoming universal."

"They focused on the hoped-for Judgment Day,
The Second Coming which was promised soon,
When every saintly and devout commune
Would be united at the entryway
Of gates of Heaven, also would 'per se'
Bring earthly power in an afternoon,
Or some short period of opportune
Resplendence that their God would thus display.
They felt their revelation would unveil
A paradise, promoting the transition
Of all the world to triumph or to loss.
But they had missed the force that would prevail,
The army of the empire and the vision
Of Constantine, the banner with the cross."

"For Jesus said he 'came to bring a sword',
Not merely passive, peaceful co-existence;
He recognized the powerful assistance
Coercion lent with an unruly horde.
For prophets are rejected or ignored
Or otherwise meet passionless resistance
Unless constraint (at not too great a distance)
Can be applied, and deference restored.
So has it been and so will always be,
That those who conquer create all the rules,
Which over time acquire the glaze of truth.
And often men of grace and honesty
Defer to those in power, often fools
Who may be kind, more often are uncouth."

"The Prophet was a moral visionary,
But also he became a man of war,
And of the two he used his scimitar
With great effect in many military
Encounters prior to the necessary
Conversion of the pagan, secular
Rough Bedouins, and in particular
The Arabs in their city-sanctuary.
The citizens of Mecca were defeated
In warfare prior to their transformation,
Before the tide of Islam rose to douse
The crude religions, and the work completed;
Crusading was the Prophet's consummation."
(May peace be on his head and in his house).

"Most people are but members of a state
As cattle are as numbers in a herd,
And both these groups have passively deferred
Unto a single leader with a trait
Enabling him to see and find the straight
Direction for a certain goal; inferred
Is acquiescence from those led, conferred
By sheep upon a goat to navigate.
But people choose republics or a prince,
And most are led by either, easily.
Majorities are eager to obey
Someone who has the power to convince
The masses, truly or dishonestly;
This is as valid now as yesterday."

"Then how is one to live successfully?
Initially, the problem is of *will* ;
No person in this world succeeds until
He dedicates himself, the *'will to be'*.
We see in Caesar, though his tyranny
Was wicked, yet his iron resolve was still
Effective when he needed to fulfill
What he envisioned as his destiny.
As cunning as a fox, and lion-fierce
He was invincible and could devour
All enemies he found within his way.
Thus no antagonist could ever pierce
His shield until he laid aside his power;
False confidence and trust led him astray."

"So what is strength? The necessary means
By which a leader's ends may be achieved;
The Medici subdued the Florentines
By brutal force, not by what they believed.
Authority is for the ones with skill
To seize it in an open competition
And use it for the good or for the ill,
It matters not; it is the acquisition
That will determine failure or success.
The winning side can then pretend to be
More virtuous, legitimate, and less
Tyrannical by pure legality.
Thus strength will always weaknesses devour
The *will to be* becomes the *will to power*."

I stepped aside from him that I might think
More clearly on the principles he taught,
And how he so completely could unlink
The virtues, honesty and truth, that ought
To guide effective action and events,
Reverse them so the principle of force
Was dominant, and afterwards dispense
Invented righteousness without remorse.
He never thought of faith, humility
Or love, forgiveness or of Christian meekness,
As anything but clutter and debris,
And all were traits that indicated weakness.
He saw the possible, but not the just,
And so I left him there, with some disgust.

THE RE-BIRTH OF MORALITY

I. The Conscience of the King

The causeway then continued free and clear
Above the gulf that split the old from new,
It tended toward the north, and there the view
Seemed more reserved and ordered, more austere.
With piety and public virtue here
The instances of anarchy were few;
Without the chaos, scholarship now grew
More solidly, less brilliant, more sincere.
Ahead I saw two alcoves near each other;
Two men were waiting, both dressed somberly,
Conversing with no sign of egotism.
They seemed an older and a younger brother,
In learning equal, complementary,
And both despising church scholasticism.

The two together possibly contained
The greatest sum of learning I had seen,
And both were equally inclined and keen
To cleanse the evils that the Church retained.
Ecclesiastical reform remained
Their object, both were thoughtful and serene,
But neither was prepared for things unseen,
The violent revolt the Church sustained.
They both protested in a quiet way,
Deploring Luther and his heresy,
And Calvin, and Loyola, their opponent.
They saw good-will and tolerance decay
Until reform and reason were not free
To serve much longer as a Church component.

The first was English and Lord Chancellor,
A man of learning, also piety;
And though he tried to balance equally
The modern world and ancient faith, therefore
Rejecting either as superior,
Preventing, by his moral honesty
Both civil and religious atrophy,
His failure served as cogent metaphor.
He served his king, but with this reservation:
That first he served the principles of God
With equity and honor, no pretension,
No faulty or deceitful variation.
The problem was the king, who raced rough-shod
Toward his desires, allowing no dissension.

His vision of *Utopia* allots
The best of everything to all, a range
Of equal benefits, which interchange
With Christian principles and allied thoughts.
But though he dreamed progressive social plots,
Defining ideal life, both new and strange,
The man of honor found he could not change,
The aging leopard not erase his spots.
He gazed into the past, before the bridge
Had made the leap from moral confidence,
As if a great enclosed protective curtain
Was lifted, canceling its heritage
Of fixed assurance; as a consequence,
A world arose where nothing now was certain.

As I approached, I felt that he was caught
Within a world developing too fast;
His mind had separated from the past
And was a model of progressive thought.
But though his open intellect had brought
Him to this modern world, there was a vast
Uneasy feeling that he was miscast,
A lack of certainty left him distraught.
For morally, enlightenment had failed;
The ancient rules had ceased to be respected,
Allowing in their place, licentiousness.
Immoral wanton cruelty assailed
His sense of worth and left him unprotected,
And all that he had lived by, valueless.

He spoke to me with quiet resignation,
"I sadly saw corruption verified,
And arrogance, the evil of self-pride,
Which changes compromise to confrontation.
Between two holy orders arbitration
Might easily have been a better guide,
Thus healing from within the great divide,
And bringing us a valid reformation.
The Church's mission must not be retarded
Nor shaped by frivolous or trifling whim,
Nor should authority of man be placed
Above the principles of God; unguarded,
The lamp of revelation will grow dim,
A thousand years of history erased."

"And so, in my official life I tried
To be a rational and honest man,
Above all with the king, an Anglican,
(A group that I had often vilified).
Despite religious tension, he relied
On my ability, which over-ran
His prejudice at first, but soon began
To be irrelevant, and set aside.
He never doubted my integrity
But here, perhaps, I went a bit too far,
With honor to the point of indiscretion.
A foe of virtue is hypocrisy,
That twists the soul into a circular
Dishonest form, unworthy of confession."

"So what is there of my experience,
That you or others might extrapolate,
Insert into your lives, avoid the fate
For which I seemed to have a poor defense?
Is there a force of nature so immense
So comprehensive that it can create
Imbalance, where there is no counterweight
And reason fades into indifference?
The guidelines of the old morality
Were never carved in granite, never etched,
Forever to remain unmodified.
There are conditions we cannot foresee
For which the principles will need be stretched
So that they do not break, or subdivide."

"If you preserve them, they will serve you well,
No matter that they seem to be submersed
Within your deepest soul, or interspersed
With lesser principles in parallel.
The time will come, so will the infidel,
The skeptic, unbeliever, those who cursed
The will of God, or otherwise reversed
The proper forms of Heaven and of Hell.
So do not let your soul be undefined,
But keep it close within you as you live;
And when this future time of trial commences
Look deep inside your heart and life to find
Within yourself, your own imperative,
And in this world, accept the consequences."

"In life you will encounter much contention,
Some conflicts you will win and some will lose.
This option may be left for you to choose:
Not triumph or defeat, but what dimension
You will allow the strife, how much dissension
Your soul accepts, how much it can excuse,
And at what point it simply will refuse
Admittance to a new, destructive tension.
The central core of faith, if firm and strong,
And tempered by a hard experience,
May bend with circumstance, but will not break;
Confronted by an arbitrary wrong
Or threatening, impious arguments,
It keeps the soul from making a mistake."

"This sturdiness of soul will not permit
The evil of the world to penetrate
Within yourself or to accumulate
To levels overwhelming, infinite,
That might compel a lesser to submit.
Beyond sustaining strength, compassionate
Integrity will trump degenerate
Behavior of the heathen and unfit.
The soul that is prepared, impervious,
Will keep all earthly evil at a distance,
Immune from every outside adversary;
It clarifies what is ambiguous,
Becomes the very center of existence,
The ultimate, eternal sanctuary."

And he himself, did this apply to him?
For life had swept him up among the stars,
Where floating free upon the very rim
Of regal power and spectaculars
The hollowness of unsupported living
Was evident among the people there.
He knew that destiny was unforgiving
And led the uncommitted to despair.
So, ready when the great descending arc
Of fate (or royal whim), had cast him down
Into disgrace, a swimmer in the dark
And rough unending sea who would not drown,
His conscious faith, prepared so carefully,
Protected him with calm serenity.

When challenged to support the English king,
As head of both the State and of the Church,
He had a binding moral wakening;
Before deciding, made a thorough search.
And looking for divine authority,
He calculated all the varied odds,
(Allowing points for royal destiny)
And could not make man's wisdom great as God's.
Profoundly pious, filled with altruism,
He faced decisions certainly rabbinic;
So though he'd come so far to humanism,
He (never indecisive or a cynic)
Declined to give approval, and instead
Refused, became a saint, and lost his head.

II. The Conscience of the Church

The next, by far the greatest humanist,
Supreme before the great religious schism,
Was dominant in his scholasticism
And well-respected by each altruist.
He was the consummate protagonist
Of those who resurrected classicism;
He moderated harsh antagonism,
Remaining an objective analyst.
He was the essence of a moderate,
Reforming church injustice from within,
And shunning any role as an aggressor.
In certain crises, forced to arbitrate
In arguments, he often would begin
By working out which evil was the lesser.

When born of an irregular relation
His future seemed far less than average;
Inventing a romantic heritage
Provided him with some alleviation.
But this did not supply the education
Which he achieved himself; with patronage
Of guardians he went, though underage,
To be a monk, without much dedication.
Perhaps his name was "Desiderius
Erasmus" with some subtle irony
Relating to his birth, because it meant
"Desired Beloved", a precarious
But hopeful label somewhat ruefully
Applied to screen or mask the accident.

Monastic life had never been his yearning,
But he believed that he could tolerate
Obedience, perhaps stay celibate,
Control the feelings of dislike concerning
Austerity, as long as he was learning.
But then he found that he could explicate
The Latin lessons and could conjugate
In Greek, and was in logic quite discerning.
No longer was the fasting worth his while,
His life within the order went downhill;
He found that he disliked the monastery,
But even then he could not reconcile
Unfinished studies, did not leave until
He finished every book in its library.

Assignment as a bishop's secretary
(The price was ordination as a priest),
Allowed him easy travel, and southeast
Was Paris, then the revolutionary
Convergence of the new contemporary
Activity opposing what had ceased
To be exclusive doctrine (or at least
Agreement was no longer necessary).
The University now proved to be
The leading (or the central) source of learning;
And new philosophies could co-exist
With old Scholastic church theology.
He found his future in the school concerning
The newer system known as "Humanist".

When Paris had no more that he could learn
He went to Italy and did the same,
Devouring all the books he found, and came
To love the life in Rome. His brief sojourn
Divided tours of England, his return
To Paris, then to Holland soon became
A way of life; he lectured to acclaim,
But almost starved on fees that he could earn.
So he became a poor itinerant
(But famous and respected) scholar who
Wrote polished Latin, passing Greek and Dutch,
And somewhat modest Hebrew; elegant
In classic style and wit, his power grew,
An influence that no one else could touch.

He fought ecclesiastical abuses
Before the Reformation did the same.
When none had heard of Martin Luther's name,
Erasmus ridiculed the priests' excuses
For selling pardons; this of course induces
Corruption in the Church, thus bringing shame
To bishops and to popes, who cannot claim
The holy life that purity produces.
His fiercest words were for monastic orders,
The pious fools who only love themselves,
Who think religion is meticulous
Attention to their ritual that borders
On pure obsession with some trifle, delves
No deeper into truth than all of us.

Like Petrarch in the past, and Cicero,
His letters (all in Latin), coveted
By scholars, princes, popes and kings, were read
Because of witty charming style, and flow
Of fresh ideas, and those of long-ago,
Combining new and classic thought, instead
Of stale Scholastic doctrines so inbred
That they no longer had the room to grow.
He lacked the modesty and gratitude
That would have served him well in trying times;
But when your friends and confidants are kings
(Of England and of Poland) and include
Philosophers and cardinals, sometimes
Humility and grace are awkward things.

But nonetheless, regardless of this pride,
He found a welcome where the mysteries
Were contemplated: universities,
Ecclesiastic courts, where popes decide
How sacred laws of God should be applied,
And how the newly found discrepancies
Could be resolved. His skill and strategies
Were humanistic virtue's greatest guide.
He had the Church's cautious benediction
By reason of his brilliant erudition,
By which he could expose each fallacy.
And yet, while lacking courage and conviction
To dominate disputes, his opposition
Was full of passionate intensity.

In Christian creed he praised simplicity,
Said truth was from the heart and not the head,
And any true religion merited
An absence of ornate theology.
All priests should demonstrate humility
And imitate the life their Master led;
Since He Himself was poor, Erasmus said
That popes themselves should live in penury.
He ridiculed the self-important pious
Who failed in Christ's commandment, "Love each other",
Predicting He would call them Pharisees
Because they showed an overwhelming bias
To love themselves instead of one another,
With vain displays of petty pieties.

He was the conscience of a generation
Throughout the continent and England too,
The modern world was making its debut
With scientific knowledge its foundation;
And ancient faith required interpretation
In order to stay relevant and true.
Because a synthesis was overdue,
He tried to find a valid explanation.
But more than that, apparently, was needed,
And this he was unable to supply;
For he had been persuasive, not aggressive
And would have intervened or interceded
In anything finesse could rectify,
But by that time the breach was too excessive.

The Reformation then became a fact.
He lived awhile in Catholic Louvain
And tried with his persuasion to contain
(He did not have the force to counteract)
The agonizing rupture of compact
United Christian doctrine, its domain
Now split in segments, none that could regain
Consensus which could keep the Church intact.
And then he lived in Basel (Protestant),
Where many there attempted to enlist
His eminence and great authority;
But though he recognized significant
Defects within the Church, as activist
For change, he chose to work more peacefully.

He praised a genuine simplicity
Of spirit, from the heart and not the head,
And thought elaborate theology
Superfluous, and better left unsaid.
His attitude was one of affirmation
That always was repelled by violence;
He hated war and fury, confrontation,
Believing in the force of common sense.
His era passed, he saw the fates dispatch
A time for courage and intolerance
And he had neither, so he could not match
The strength of Luther, nor his arrogance.
And faced with these, he bent (as he had feared),
Became irrelevant, and disappeared.

The men upon the bridge had tried to span
The great transition reasonably, with peace;
But fraud, corruption and deceit began
To fill the moral chasm and increase,
To overwhelm a just conciliation.
The archway had protected them awhile
From anarchy, until their dedication
Was crushed by force they could not reconcile.
Each in his way had failed, and paid the price,
Irrelevance, disgrace or death was dealt
By fate; and as they made their sacrifice,
Beneath their elevation heard and felt
Confused ordeals of struggle, loss and flight
Where blind fanatic armies clashed by night.

THE TIGER

Then as they slowly faded from my sight
As earlier they had from world attention,
I looked ahead, confessing apprehension,
Beyond the place the bridge, from all its height
Came down to earth again, to re-unite
With solid ground; beyond the arch-extension
It seemed to merge into a new dimension,
Immensely open, level, filled with light.
A giant meadow, limitless and new
As bright as if a sun had just emerged,
Provided clarity with its assistance.
And in this open space a scattered crew
Of men in ones and twos that often merged
Discussed again the questions of existence.

There were so many (standing randomly
Or wandering in groups to intersections
Where they would interchange a few reflections
Then wander off again divergently),
That I could not imagine how to see
Each individual, or gain directions
By conversation; making such connections
Seemed very hard, with their mobility.
Because I could not spend much time with any,
I audited the ones that looked involved;
And some seemed wise, but some were just absurd,
Yet none the less, I listened to as many
As I could tolerate, and then resolved
To summarize the things that I had heard.

The vastness of the scope of modern thought
Was difficult for me to comprehend.
Philosophy was able to transcend
The narrow limits that the Church had taught;
And knowledge that the scientists had brought
Was now incorporated, thus a blend
Of old and new ideas (which might offend
The older clerics) was what they now sought.
Without ecclesiastical restraint,
The mind was free, no longer limited
By fixed conclusions it must always meet.
Belief expanded (not without complaint)
And formed new systems that the bigoted
Dismissed or just ignored in self-deceit.

Philosophy developed secular
Directions, and withdrew from absolute
Dependence on the pious (but astute)
Monastic brothers in particular.
Its language turned into vernacular,
And paralleled the Renaissance pursuit
Of widely ranging knowledge; resolute
And free inquiry now was regular.
Among these figures: Bacon, Hobbes, Descartes
Who entered now their new and modern eras
Defining all the world by mathematics,
Concerned with substance and its counterpart,
Material, dismissing those chimeras,
Ideals and universals, as erratics.

Now free of theological constraint
A wide diffuse inquiry came about,
In which it was permissible to doubt
The ancient ignorance without restraint.
And many could absorb without complaint
The scientific concepts coming out;
Not all were heretics, some were devout,
But not a single one became a saint.
Among them, the enigma, Thomas Hobbes,
Who was suspicious of both love and hate,
Distrusting men as individuals,
But even more collectively as mobs.
Obsessed by fear of anarchy as fate
He saw men as ferocious animals.

If men in nature lived like bees or ants,
Co-operating in the hive or nest
With no desire except for what is best
Collectively for all inhabitants,
We would not need the specious covenants
Or social contracts which are manifest
Between the common people who detest
Or fear each other, with intolerance.
The chief of all desires, self-preservation,
Prevents communal links to friends and brothers.
"Preserving liberty" means they resort,
With overwhelming drive for domination,
To brutal strife of all against all others,
And life is only "nasty, brutish, short".

He was empirical and mathematic
(So rare to find them both in one, those days),
A guest of Galileo, could appraise
Both science and religion, each dogmatic.
He carefully constructed an emphatic
Material proposal that obeys
The laws of mathematics and displays
All mechanistic mandates, each pragmatic.
His universe was based on constant motion
Of particles and bodies, which colliding,
Made accidental causes and effects.
But this did not leave room for any notion
Of independent will, or thoughts providing
A basis for judicious intellects.

For him, the mind was motion in the brain,
There was no space for an immortal soul;
A goodly motion (pleasant) is our goal,
But unsuccessful movement causes pain.
Each individual must ascertain
If pleasure, which is good, will thus control
His life, or will discomfort play a role;
If pain is bad, how much can each sustain?
This is the basis of morality,
Which is not absolute but relative,
Depending on one's nature at each minute;
What pleases one man, and accordingly
Is virtuous, might not be positive
In any other, might have evil in it.

When God Himself gave movement to all things,
This was the very essence of creation.
And He still rules the world, by acclamation
Through surrogates, divinely destined kings.
For out of action in the brain there springs
Opposed desires and loathing, activation
Of what will pass for thought, deliberation,
But not the power that *will* or *freedom* brings.
The task of man is first to understand
The laws of motion, thus the universe;
And with his social contract to avoid
The wickedness of anarchy, demand
That all obey authority (perverse,
Unjust or absolute) or be destroyed.

And free of superstition to the last,
In many ways his thinking was unique;
He shattered all the systems of the past,
Philosophy (Scholastic and/or Greek),
With reasoning both logical and clear,
And all he wrote was understandable.
His basic premises were all sincere
(If somewhat harsh), there was one obstacle:
He tended to omit some awkward facts
So openly that no one misconstrued;
His arguments were vigorous but crude,
Debates were settled with a battle-axe.
Reviewing all his work, I could not find
A reason to retain him in my mind.

THE

GOD-INTOXICATED MAN

Then there were also Bacon and Descartes,
Sequestering the new philosophy
From all religious faith as totally
Irreconcilable and set apart.
Belief was purely feeling from the heart,
Unproveable; the other faculty
Was sheltered in the mind, where it could be
Devoted to pure reason from the start.
By this they meant that laws could be induced
By study of specific things and actions,
And these could build a mental diagram
And universal principles unloosed.
The solid objects faded to abstractions,
The mind remained: "I think, therefore, I am".

And also in these groupings, Berkeley, Hume,
And Leibnitz with his *monads*, and John Locke,
All grappled with new learning run amok;
Debate and logic filled the mental room
Produced by freedom from the moral gloom
Of centuries of managed thought. The shock
Of liberated views would soon unlock
A controversy likely to consume
Itself. Each interacted with the others,
But quarreled with the metaphysics seen
Another way; they always were at odds
Concerning concepts, and with one another's
Descriptions, "What exactly did he mean?"
They were like pagans, all with clashing gods.

Although one Scotsman, David Hume, was there,
He was uncertain of his own existence;
Reality itself required assistance.
By his perception, if he saw a chair,
The chair existed; if he then would stare
Away from it, perhaps into the distance,
The chair would disappear, and his insistence
Made him a skeptic, ending in despair.
To those who said that God was just aloof
(Remote, withdrawn, but possibly in view),
He said this was a fanciful conceit;
He had not *seen* this God, there was no proof.
Ideas within his mind alone were true,
Philosophy was thus a dead-end street.

I needed some relief from negative
Interpretations of the universe,
My view that Hobbes or Hume (or both) were worse
Than reassuring and affirmative
I thought was certain; as a way to live
Their models seemed the absolute reverse
Of what I sought, I needed to disperse
Depression by a new alternative.
I sought advice from others, was directed
To one who sat apart, the opposite
Of most of those whom I had interviewed.
As I approached, I easily detected
That he was gracious and considerate,
And yet contented in his solitude.

Baruch (or Benedict) Spinoza, who
Was born a Jew, but excommunicated,
Had found that his philosophy was hated
By Christians also, they would misconstrue
His doctrine of pervasive God into
The atheism they abominated;
(Ironic, since he said we are related
Constituents of what is pure and true).
This unity pervades the universe
And all, including men, are part of God.
Since everything in life is consecrated,
There is no latitude for any curse,
And their antagonism seems more odd
Since he was called "the God-intoxicated."

His problem started with an open mind
Which led him, after study, into doubt.
The Scriptures and the Talmud seemed throughout
To show irregularities inclined
To new interpretation; he could find
In scholars like Maimonides devout
But skeptical uncertainties about
Some doctrines that to them seemed mis-aligned.
Then he himself had added systematic
Review of sciences, geometry
And mathematics, based on reasoning,
But did not cultivate the diplomatic
And tactful skill, or even modesty
That would have mitigated everything.

In contrast to his rumored "atheism"
Was *substance* (God) in body and in mind,
And all its attributes could be combined
Into an absolute idealism.
This entity, this God, this organism,
Pervasive through the cosmos, was defined
As single and eternal, unconfined,
Autonomous beyond our criticism.
But we can recognize His attributes:
A thought within our mind is one dimension,
But there are others, substances like trees
Or human forms, whatever constitutes
The world of thought, the world of things, extension
Throughout the world, and all infinities.

This "substance" of the world is like a shield,
With different designs on either side.
On one, the shape of body is applied,
The other, etched or carved and then annealed,
Is where the mind and thinking is revealed.
Examining the object, we decide
To look at either face, not subdivide
The substance, which itself is firmly sealed.
So every object in the universe,
The stars and water, wind and stones and man,
Are part of God, but also every thought;
The forces, processes that intersperse
To cause the working out of God's own plan,
Will make these objects function as they ought.

Since everything is God, thus pantheistic,
What can be evil, harmful, false or bad?
Or ever give us pain, or make us sad?
Assuredly not God's own altruistic
Control, nor is this God at all deistic.
The errors men may make are myriad,
But all related to one source, iron-clad;
An ignorance, beliefs that are simplistic.
Obscure, inadequate ideas will fail,
Relying on the senses and perception
Or on imagination (incorrect),
Will lead to struggle, but to no avail.
The understanding minds, without exception
Will show their love of God through intellect.

The metaphysical is preparation
For righteous conduct and philosophy
Which comes from living wisely, so we see
The basic unity, our correlation
With God's eternal will; self-preservation
Will govern conduct, but with clarity.
By *understanding* we may choose to be
United with the sum of God's creation.
A strong man hates no one, and is not proud,
Endeavors to repay contempt with love,
Desiring nothing for himself which he
Would not desire that mankind be allowed.
By *reason* he arises far above
A thoughtless life to touch eternity.

So man can touch, but not participate;
The body, though a form of God, obeys
The laws of science, those which delegate
The limitations that the world displays.
But mind and spirit, equally a mode
Of God (the only substance), cannot die;
And even though their visible abode
(The body), changes, souls intensify,
Continue as a part of God, and share
(Though not as individuals) the essence
Of holy substance present everywhere
That lights the universe with incandescence.
There is one truth that no one can avoid,
A part of man can never be destroyed.

I recognized in him a noble soul,
Beloved in his personality,
And never known to argue or cajole;
He lived, as well as wrote, philosophy.
Reviled by Jews, and by the Christians hated
As Satan, or the very Antichrist
He then (by both) was excommunicated,
But living as a saint for him sufficed.
Though I admired him as a moral man
Who faced each curse of Deuteronomy
As if he might be Job, more patient than
A lesser person lacking gravity,
Reviewing all his life I ought to add
That I could never live the way he had.

THE ABSTRACT THEORIST

Encountering the French, at first Voltaire,
And his compatriot and friend, Rousseau
(A friend at first, and later more a foe),
I found myself enlightened by this pair,
Who valued human freedom everywhere.
But finally their arguments would grow
Until their insults, given *quid pro quo*
Resulted in a farcical affair.
A famous earthquake lately had occurred;
They quarreled over theological
Significance: Was God in charge of things?
Was he distracted elsewhere, or deferred
His intervention? Was this doctrinal
Reprisal in the form of sufferings?

These two, Voltaire, Rousseau, were inconsistent
Throughout their lives, and changes of position
Were always common, each found ammunition
To disagree with those both near and distant.
On his own virtue each remained insistent,
And prejudiced, there was no recognition
Of tolerance in either's disposition;
And harmony, of course, was non-existent.
Aside from earthquakes, the morality
Of modern, worldly plays was in dispute;
Because Voltaire had written them Rousseau,
Adopting Puritan antipathy
To pleasure, labeled drama dissolute
And souls of playwrights useless, vain and low.

Religion, too; Voltaire (a Catholic)
Believed in God, was not an atheist,
But did not think theology should twist
The purity of Jesus into slick
Manipulative rites and rhetoric.
Rousseau was born a solid Calvinist,
But as a secret life-long pragmatist,
Converted/Reconverted double-quick.
But even though enlightened and romantic,
I could not profit from their explanations,
For both were troubled by their inconsistence,
And often seemed as if consumed by frantic
Defenses, reasoning, and accusations;
As I went on, they bickered in the distance.

The later Germans then appeared to me,
Like Hegel, Fichte, Schopenhauer, Schelling;
The thing that seemed to be their most compelling
Relation was their lack of unity.
Although they shared the common legacy
Derived from Kant, and largely paralleling
The century's idealistic swelling,
I could not find a common harmony.
Each was a critic and antagonistic,
Each theory dissected and disputed,
And all their mental spider-webs so dense
They finally became surrealistic.
Their logic was abstract, so convoluted,
How could I know which one would make some sense?

So finally I chose a single one
As representative of all the rest,
Not necessarily because the best
Was obvious at first; comparison
Was superficial, really there were none
On first inspection who seemed likeliest.
But there was one who, somewhat overdressed,
Precise and neat, was yet no simpleton.
The rumor was he taught the middle class
Of students ("Dunces are beyond all aid,
While geniuses will help themselves") and so
I trusted him as guide through this morass
With thoughtful lessons so I might evade
The consequence of what I did not know.

He sat upon a bench, with one end clear,
And offered all the other space to me;
"I have until exactly half-past-three,
Then will like Cinderella, disappear.
When citizens of Königsberg can hear
My cane upon the paving-stones, they see
The time upon their clocks, and all agree
To set them daily as I reappear."
Diminutive in stature, almost frail
(A single ancient servant stood behind
And held a large umbrella, just in case),
He dressed correctly, true in each detail
As if the facets of his life aligned
Together in a regulated space.

"A warning first," he said, "I'm thought to be
By far a better teacher than a writer,
To this each critic and quotation-citer
And student-readers certainly agree.
So if you will allow me, graciously,
To offer you an outline, somewhat slighter,
And not so deep and comprehensive, lighter
Than what is in my books, a summary.
For we should keep things simple, should we not?
Speak only what analysis distils,
For there are wordy and undisciplined
Philosophers, who mystify somewhat;
They live in highest towers and on hills
Where one can find warm air and blowing wind."

"They say my metaphysics is oblique,
But you must understand how I arrived
At ethics which for centuries survived,
Whose influence is even now unique.
By reason I devised a new technique
To shape awareness which has been derived
From sensory experience, revived
And then subjected to a new critique.
The only things we absolutely know
Are what we hear and see and touch and feel,
And we are confident of scientific
Phenomena upon their own plateau;
But on another plane our minds reveal
And shape ideas both certain and specific."

"And even though you've learned the truths of science
(Which no one doubts, they need no new defendant),
There are some other concepts, called 'transcendent';
These go beyond our knowledge in defiance
Of reason and our senses, their alliance
Creates a moral truth which independent,
But parallel with science is ascendant
As virtue is with God in full compliance.
And this transcendent truth is necessary
For living well, the basis of morality
And counteracting human skepticism.
For though we cannot prove by ordinary
Experience and reason immortality,
Yet we should look at this with optimism."

"Since value is the essence of a soul,
Then, we must act as if it does exist
And cannot perish, cannot be dismissed
By time or death, which we cannot control.
This universal reason has a goal
Beyond the scope of any scientist
And contradicting every nihilist:
To make our lives complete and perfect, whole.
An outer world is made by a Creator
Who also forms the soul, the majesty
Of man, through independent will alone.
He also acts as final arbitrator
Of all our moral questions, therefore He
Is necessary, even though unknown."

"By reason we can limit skepticism
Which recognizes only what's perceived,
And isolated things which are believed,
But have no real existence; nihilism
Applied to thoughts of God is atheism.
And if there is one thing that I've achieved,
The freedom of man's choice has been retrieved,
And all of us are saved from fatalism.
For God is absolutely necessary
Beyond the need for any evidence.
He validates the freedom of our actions
And makes our virtue, which is voluntary
Significant; through these unforced events
Our lives become much more than mere abstractions."

He spent some minutes seeming to rehearse
And organize his thoughts, and then began:
"Before beginning to construct a plan
Which might (or not) explain the universe,
We should examine changing and diverse
Varieties of knowledge, those which can
Be useful and utilitarian,
Opposed to forms which can mislead, or worse.
Two worlds exist, somewhat in parallel,
The first is based upon experience,
Specifically on physical sensation;
We see an object, but we cannot tell
Its essence, character or consequence
Without an intellect, our mind's creation."

"The next plateau, or intersecting plane,
Derivative from all experience
But shaped within our minds with confidence
And thus allowing us to ascertain
The meaning of sensations we obtain,
Consists of networks drawn from evidence
Converted from this worldly turbulence
By reason to a pattern in our brain.
This sequence or Idea is what we know,
And thus we form a concept, explanation
Of things that otherwise would always be
Unrecognized within our minds, although
They would exist outside our contemplation
Without a meaning to us inwardly."

"A man must act as if this world exists,
In order to preserve integrity
And moral excellence; accordingly
An action that is virtuous consists
Of what is universal and enlists
Inclusiveness for its validity.
It is a principle for all to see
And follow if they can, as activists.
Imagine that you are the Prussian king
(More autocratic ones could not be found),
And you could order all subordinates
To imitate your life in everything;
Would virtue still be evident, profound
And uniform as it disseminates?"

"Commandments of the king, imperatives,
Must be obeyed, however trivial
By everyone, thus categorical.
And afterward, the state or nation lives
In unity with clear affirmatives,
Or else confusion and illogical
Chaotic tumult if unethical
Or foolish rules appear as negatives.
They live in universal harmony
If virtue is within the inspiration
The king extends to customary law.
In contrast, they will suffer endlessly,
Destruction and disgrace their condemnation
If his idea contains a fatal flaw."

"Now substitute your reasoned God for 'king';
He gives His orders to the universe,
And is the Source (for better or for worse),
The One who is the cause of everything.
This framework is, of course, quite challenging,
To touch, to see, to feel will not rehearse
This new demand: to totally immerse
The spirit in a new awakening.
Though reason only vaguely comprehends
How virtual reality persists
And concepts have a life just as they should,
All virtue, all morality depends
On *if* this kind of world (and God) exists,
And one's belief directs one to the good."

"So you must live upon this second plane
Where virtue, life and God are infinite;
For these conceptions are pre-requisite
If reason's view of things is to remain
Pre-eminent in all of life's domain.
Then freedom of the human will can fit
Into this universe and thus permit
Responsibilities that lives contain.
But there is still a higher form of truth
Than offered by our own intelligence.
The moral law within us guarantees
Immunity from foolishness of youth;
Maturity of values, competence
Are universal righteous indices."

"The first of all our problems is to know
What may be true in life, and what illusion;
We must not start our quest in blind confusion,
Mistakes are weights we seldom can outgrow.
Beginning on an errant path we go
Great distances in utter self-delusion
Before awakening to this conclusion:
Naïveté may be our greatest foe.
We must admit, believe or just accept
Existence of 'the-thing-which-is-itself',
The outer world (outside the mind) which might
Not truly be, might not exist, except
As seen by reason, objects on a shelf,
Invisible in darkness, as at night."

"Accepting this construction, how are we
To live our lives with honor, day by day?
Protect against disorder and convey
A placid spirit through adversity?
We must admit the human mind to be
Creator of its own distinctive way,
Conforming to itself alone, mainstay
Of all we know or think deductively.
For space and time (although they may exist)
Cannot be known without the human reason,
Reality is what we recognize.
Outside our minds, the world may be dismissed,
Ephemeral as any fleeting season,
And vanishing without a compromise."

"So we must recognize the moral law
Requiring acts be done with good intent,
Avoiding selfish gain or blandishment
Or ostentation or an equal flaw.
Not even a result that one foresaw
Of happiness or pain, benevolent,
Unfortunate or adverse, if well-meant
Revokes or causes virtue to withdraw.
And so, the only absolutely good
Reliable and constant moral thing
In all the world remains the purity
Of human will, conforming as it should
To consciousness of duty, promising
To act, within the law, assertively."

"The moral rule is this: that every act
You might consider or perform may be
Extended as a universal key
By which to judge if virtue is intact.
Expanded from the simple to abstract,
If all perform your action equally
And it retains its authenticity
Then it is good, in theory and in fact.
But there is something more, for you must treat
Humanity, yourself or any other,
Forever as an end and not a means
For any other goal; if self-conceit
Might tempt a purpose which would harm another,
The basic moral law then intervenes."

"But know, responsibility is yours,
For you are free, and can do what you will.
The consequences, whether good or ill
Belong to you alone, and this ensures
That meaningful morality endures,
Not drowned in uniform despair, but still
Surpassing laws of nature to fulfill
The ethics ordinary life obscures.
But man can not become completely good
Within a lifetime, immortality
Is therefore necessary for the soul
To satisfy the moral law. It should
Achieve perfection, but not easily;
A bridge is needed, God fulfills that role."

"Though virtue and morality would seem
To merit fortune, joy and happiness,
Reality will force us to confess
That often life has quite a different theme.
The virtuous will have their self-esteem
Severely tested as they feel distress
When evil prospers, rectitude much less,
(Discrepancies can sometimes be extreme).
When righteousness and pleasure should be found
Together, but too often they are not,
Our fragile souls have need of sanctuary,
And footings for our moral lives, a sound
And stable base (which worldly life forgot);
This is the reason God is necessary."

This was the end of what he would disclose,
As much (he sensed) as I could comprehend:
An integrated system to defend
Morality and choice (free-will) that goes
Beyond whatever observation shows,
A system that by nature would transcend
The mechanistic world, and thus its end,
Defeating hopelessness if so I chose.
But this would be enough, if I believed
And saw the absolute necessity
Of things not proven, but still surely there.
This universe of reason was conceived
That we might live both morally and free,
Avoiding all potential for despair.

The cloudy German sky had turned to mist,
His servant spread the great umbrella out,
And then he rose to go; there was no doubt
This one supremely abstract theorist
Reverted to a strict traditionist.
Defenses he could never live without
Lay in predictable secure, devout
Adherence to routines he never missed.
It was the middle of the afternoon,
His daily walk was due, despite the rain.
Disliking all erratics and unknowns,
He bowed and slowly disappeared, and soon
I only heard the tapping of his cane
So like a clock upon the paving stones.

He said, when I had offered, "No one goes
Along with me". His constitutional
Contained a single categorical
Imperative: that breathing through the nose
Alone provided cleaner air, and those
Who tried conversing found that casual
Bronchitis might occur; his ritual
Prevented more infections than one knows.
This magic was more potent than physicians
Protecting such a fragile, frail physique,
And though he wrestled mentally with weighty
Conceptions based on logic, superstitions
Were just as good for him; despite critique,
He lived in stable health 'till he was eighty.

The intricate and spiral reasoning
Which he conceived and wrote and then revised
Throughout one-half his lifetime did not bring
A simple thought that could be memorized.
Despite his intricate complexity
In which so many brilliant minds have drowned,
His ethics proved (without hyperbole)
In all of modern thought the most profound.
The man himself seemed immunized to strife,
A servant of predictable routine,
Without imagination in his life,
Where controversy could not intervene.
And yet the synthesis which he achieved
Has not been matched by any yet conceived.

All humans have a need to classify
Ideas and concepts, personalities
In categories, most of which comply
With simple patterns, understood with ease.
Irregularities, uncomfortable,
Distracting to the ordinary mind
May represent a weighty obstacle
To comprehension for the non-aligned.
There is an honest value to simplicity,
Consistency almost a requisite;
Yet this philosopher in his complexity
Was vastly different, he would not fit
Completely into any of these boxes,
One of the world's enduring paradoxes.

COMMITMENT AND INDIFFERENCE

As I progressed, an even greater flock
Appeared, and some had wide- divergent names
Like Unamuno, Nietzsche, William James,
And Russell, Santayana, Bergson, Locke,
Each one distinct, and each a stumbling block
(With affirmations, claims and counterclaims)
To harmony; with language that inflames,
Discussions always seem to run amok.
But there were others, Spencer, Dewey, Mill,
Who sometimes were more civilized, and yet,
The factions would regroup and re-align;
All those debating fate against free-will
As governing behavior owed a debt
To Auguste Comte and Ludwig Wittgenstein.

I saw a smaller group that stood apart
Discussing levels of experience;
"Objective truth depends on common sense,
Religious faith is felt within the heart,
Unhappiness becomes a conscious art
That, shared by God and man without pretense
Exalts identity and reverence,"
Thus, Kirkegaard and Heidegger and Sartre.
"Self-knowledge is essential for each man,
A tragic figure in a finite world,
That offers only hindrance and resistance.
Awareness of identity still can
Prevent those limits which have always swirled
Around the essence that is man's existence."

But they were all obsessed with suffering,
And with the evil that is all around,
Pervasive in the world and so profound
It is beyond the thought of vanquishing.
Thus only active consciousness can bring
Redemption and the freedom from unsound
And meaningless experience; the ground
Beneath existence is *awakening*.
When he becomes aware, a man can choose
A firm commitment to a higher level,
Surpassing childish things he will outgrow.
Accepting widespread evil is to lose;
Since man cannot annihilate the devil,
His ultimate is freedom to say "No".

This presentation was for me one-sided,
And selfish in its total concentration
On individuals and their relation,
Commitment to one's self, the undivided
Awareness of one's singleness that guided
One's pathway to the true affiliation
Of self and God, and final affirmation
Of his own fate, which he himself decided.
But I did not agree that suffering,
Concern with evil, and such negative
Obsessions such as death's necessity
Should constitute the whole, the everything
In one's philosophy; I wished to live
With more than mere despair and agony.

Although their emphasis on deviation
Of true commitment from indifference,
Heroic action from coincidence,
And on assertiveness and affirmation
Was worthy, and required no explanation
(And never any shame or penitence),
I was distressed by evil's prominence,
And agony, which echoed flagellation.
Pervasive evil could not be redeemed,
Courageous opposition was a mark
Of resolution only, not of love
Or faith or generosity which seemed
To change despair into a colored arc
That rose from earth into the sky above.

There were some contrasts to this pessimism
Which permeated Existentialists,
For some insisted that a God exists
Rejecting atheistic fatalism.
But most retained a healthy skepticism
About a Deity which, prejudiced
Against or for an entity, assists
With intervention and in activism.
For Martin Buber, science and mechanics
Reduced humanity, with loss of self,
Increasing evil, wasting human souls;
With weaker strength of character, one panics
As if the world has pushed one off a shelf
Into a void, with strange and helpless roles.

Some kept their view of God, but re-defined
Their vision to an "Ultimate Concern",
Or "Ground of Being" which would overturn
Theistic features, earlier designed
To guarantee salvation to mankind
By giving laws that everyone must learn,
Extending paradise to those who earn
The privilege, on leaving life behind.
The older image, now discredited
By losing much of its symbolic force,
Became irrelevant, to be replaced
(By Tillich) with a higher form instead;
This serves mankind as ultimate resource
In which realities of life are based.

And God, who gives no artificial Law
Became ubiquitous, imperative,
In which participation as we live
Prevents anxiety, the basic flaw
In every man who clearly looked and saw
That life flows out, like water through a sieve,
And loss is certain, nothing can forgive
The fact that all existence must withdraw.
Involvement in this higher God returns
Us to ourselves, with greater confidence,
And endless dialogue, which, understood,
Submerges fear, and all of our concerns
For God's reality, and in immense
And personal release, for God is good.

Then I found balance in the "Ich und Du",
That recognized humanity-made-less
By hollow science and the world's duress
Which caused impersonal unfeeling, new
Encroachment on identity, and grew
Into a form of evil; this distress
The "I" must counteract, and so repress
The loss of dignity that might ensue.
But balanced with regaining of our own
Humanity, the "Thou" requires of us
That equally attention must be shown
To other individuals, and thus
We will become aware of all uniqueness,
Affirming strength and compensating weakness.

ILLUMINATION,

COMPLETION OF THE CYCLE

I thought perhaps my journey was complete,
I was again near where I had begun;
I wondered if my enterprise was done
Or if there was some part I must repeat.
I was not willing to admit defeat,
And yet I had no sense that I had won;
Of all the intellects I'd met, not one
Provided guidance as I'd hoped to meet.
The year was further gone, the leaves vermilion,
The color of approaching fall and death.
When all is closing, all must be in order;
And then I saw the luminous pavilion,
But only, now, through fog upon my breath,
As chilling air announced the winter's border.

Still self-possessed, they waited there for me
On my return, my guides to human thought,
To values which so many minds had sought
Throughout the sweeping curve of history.
With understanding and with sympathy
They sensed that lessons which I had been taught
Were insufficient for my needs, and ought
To be enhanced, for my serenity.
I saw again the small ironic smile
Acknowledging that they had limitations
And could not guarantee my satisfaction;
For knowledge often fails to reconcile
Validity with one's anticipations,
Or separate the real from pure abstraction.

"Now *wisdom* is another thing", they said,
"For this depends upon maturity,
Augmenting to a generous degree
Whatever knowledge you have heard or read.
With this perspective, judgment rules instead
Of blind acceptance of a theory
Which may or may not prove a fallacy,
But easily might be discredited.
A child is able to absorb some facts
And then declaim what he has memorized,
Young men are famous for their brilliancy,
Which often leads them into foolish acts
That cause their lives to go in ill-advised
Directions, and their souls to atrophy."

"Parameters of life are never learned
Without a long and hard experience,
And those who seek an easy way, dispense
With time to be invested, unconcerned
To pay a certain price, will be returned
To start again. If not, the consequence:
An unclear essence marked by turbulence;
A strong and stable life is always earned.
But even those who take this complex road,
Apply themselves to learn just who they are,
And how they fit into the universe,
May not achieve the goal they feel they're owed.
Enlightenment, at times irregular,
May prove elusive, difficult, or worse."

"But you know all these things that we have said,
For you have made a gallant effort, and
Deserve to recognize and understand
The links the life that you inherited
Must create with the past, with times ahead,
With all around you; whether God has planned
A peaceful outcome or a reprimand
Depends on whether you have been misled.
And as you know, the road is convoluted,
Directions vague and often ill-defined;
Diverse ideas are factors that forbid
Coherent understanding, undisputed.
Now tell us what is clear within your mind."
I said that I would try, and so I did.

"As I remember, this is what I've learned:
The mysteries of life, some quite complex
Will never plague or trouble, never vex
A mind remaining empty, unconcerned.
And some, those truly frightened, those who turned
Away by conscious effort or reflex
From problems that seemed certain to perplex,
Preferred an easy faith they had not earned.
But those with courage faced uncertainty,
Acknowledging, but then rejecting fear,
Resolving that they would confront confusion,
Accepting that there is no guarantee
Of certainty; their effort was sincere,
They tried to live their lives without illusion."

"A great philosopher (the very first),
Repudiated unexamined lives
(And also non-essential shrewish wives,
He did not make it clear which one was worst).
His name was Socrates, and he conversed
With colleagues on a problem that derives
From common human fears, and still survives,
A quandary that no one has dispersed.
But he was willing to attempt the task
Though it consumed his life and many more,
For he proposed to find which men are wise
(And which are not); expressly he would ask
Those questions that endeavored to explore
Scenarios that he could analyze."

"I do remember all the varied schools
Which followed closely that of Socrates,
A spectrum of ideas, and some of these
Were surely wise, but others came from fools.
In classic times, there seemed to be no rules
Requiring scorn of all antitheses,
(So great a cynic as Diogenes
Could live in peace with those he ridicules).
Amid this tolerance, I wandered by
The school of Plato (or Idealists),
Sophistic thought and its derivative,
The Skeptics, those I could not classify,
And Aristotle with his scientists;
They taught me ways to think, not how to live."

"And then there came the rigid, inelastic
Theology (with reason secondary),
Proposed by academics who would vary
In details only, overall Scholastic
Beliefs did not provide enthusiastic
Variety of thought; the necessary
Objective: to promote the doctrinary
Conformity that was ecclesiastic.
They started with their pre-ordained conclusion,
Then reasoned backwards toward reality,
Explaining what they all already knew.
Attempting to avoid the sure confusion
When facts collided with theology,
They tried to make the mystical seem true."

"I sensed that they were preaching to their choir
And I myself had yet to be converted,
So all the efforts that the monks exerted
Were more than simple pilgrims would require.
I sought a lucid faith that could inspire
An honest life, and needed a concerted
Belief or principle, but they inverted
Restraint and clarity to their desire.
And this, a complex doctrine and theology
(Essential only for the dedicated),
Thus kept them busy writing and defending
Arcane hypotheses of eschatology
And other esoteric concepts, stated
In language far beyond my comprehending."

"So I moved on, into the newer thought
Where final outcomes were not pre-ordained,
And therefore inner logic not so strained,
To see how modern thinkers lived and taught,
And what new vital insights they had brought
To those who sought enlightenment; they gained
Variety and freedom, but maintained
The lack of clarity that I had sought.
Of all the people of this great re-birth
A few I could admire (but others not),
And none were paragons of vital living;
For some had morals of decisive worth
With little confidence, or had forgot
That bullies in this world are unforgiving."

"The best of them were lacking in conviction,
And facing passionate intensity
Could not prevail, defend or even be
Protected from a ruinous affliction.
This simple want, this critical restriction
Prevented living as assertively
As I would wish in any way for me,
And many such had shown this contradiction.
So as the Church's moral strength diminished
And discipline gave way to anarchy,
The void was filled by science and by force,
One neutral morally, the other finished
In cynical deceit, hypocrisy;
And both were insufficient for my course."

"This modern world was free of prejudice
And open to unlimited debate;
Each individual could advocate
By some incredible analysis
A perfect, but unlikely edifice,
Conclusions that would surely culminate
In strong reaction, some would integrate
These notions in their own new synthesis.
Consensus of opinion was surrendered,
But clarity did not emerge, along
With free discussion came its opposite.
A muddle of perceptions was engendered,
Which were essentially, although not *wrong,*
Confused, and on the whole inadequate."

"And none were simple, unadorned, direct;
They might be used for mental exercise
Demanding focused thought to analyze,
But seldom clear and easy, circumspect.
They all were comprehensive and correct
(Within their own internal logic), wise,
But could not be extended to advise
A searching, uncommitted intellect.
As one example, *monads*, windowless
Eternal units of a primal force
Made up the world, each body and its soul;
These units disconnect and coalesce
As God, the clearest one, the only source
Creates the other units of the Whole."

"Although this might be clear to Gottfried Leibnitz,
It certainly was never clear to me.
And even if, with flawless harmony
This form, (so perfect, polished, as befits
The synthesis of unrelated bits
Into a splendid structure, unity
Created by angelic artistry)
Were real, I could not see the benefits.
For I was looking for a clear directive
For moral guidance, and this complication
However balanced and compatible,
Could never serve or even be effective
For ethical or moral correlation;
Complexity remained an obstacle."

"For after study, this is what I knew:
Philosophers build castles in the air
With fragile stairways climbing up to where
The balance and the tension hold, while new.
And they are beautiful, encased with dew,
A shining symmetry suspended there;
Back-lit with early light, they still can bear
Illusions that they might be really true.
But filaments that link reality
To such creations are too delicate
To tolerate a touch that even slightly
Disturbs their equilibrium. To be
Made brittle by the sun and then beset
By common sense will cause collapse, and rightly."

"As Grecian capitals became ornate
From simple true beginnings, so convictions
Commence as pure ideas, but then restrictions
And petty supplements accumulate.
Explaining all these meanings will create
More quandaries, and even contradictions;
Elaborate constructions (nearly fictions)
Become too much to grasp, and much too late.
By then, what had begun as sensible,
And possible for all to understand
In all its basic truth and relevance,
Has grown, become incomprehensible,
With early lucid images now banned
Or suffocated by extravagance."

"The essence of all truth, simplicity,
Seems, in effect, impossible to find
In all religion and philosophy
Where clarity and candor are maligned.
In mathematics, numbers which are prime
Exist unfactored, in themselves, alone.
In physics, mass and energy and time
Are concepts with an essence of their own.
So when the mind begins to analyze
Itself, integrity, and ways to live,
It must abbreviate and crystallize
And be condensed to be definitive.
So, likewise, principles of faith are good
According to how well they're understood."

So then I left their warm secure retreat;
The two of them had earned their Camelot,
Achieving resolution, now complete
Together with their love, and I had not.
I had been given visions of the grail
But still forbidden to achieve it yet,
For all my energy had seemed to fail
In finding what I had aspired to get:
Illumination of a way to see
Myself related in my soul and mind,
And to the outside world; this clarity
Was still elusive, I had yet to find
That clear and open place where nothing mars
The brilliance of the sun and all the stars.

End of Part II of "Sacred Verses"